Mixed Messages:

When Upbringing
and Life Clash

Maurice Williamson

Hudson Books

To Roderick,
Thanks for your support!
Oscar Trump

DEDICATION

/.\.\

My house always rang with the harmonies of the Spinners. Felipe Wynn's majestic crooning woke everyone during my father's Saturday morning record playing ritual. 'Mighty Love' would play as my father would, well, dance and we would look at him as if he were a museum exhibit. He would heartily invite us, my sisters and me, to join him in dancing. We would speed by him, just out of his grasp and laugh at his antics as we followed the aroma of bacon my mother was preparing.

During the ballads, my father would go to his crate and extract such artists as B.B. King, Ray Charles and Oscar Brown, Jr. He wanted to keep the tempo upbeat. However, there was one song the Spinners sang that would render my father motionless, introspective and reflective. He would just sit in his chair and shake his head. An occasional "Sing it, boy" or "Tell 'em about it" would dart from his mouth. The song was 'Living just a little, Laughing just a little'. I never knew I had memorized that song until its lyrics resounded in my mind during my termination ordeal with the DEA. The power of repetition is amazing. "Living just a little, laughing just a little ain't easy." I found that to be true.

I do not feel myself a martyr nor do I want sympathy. There need not be an investigation into how the Justice Department conducts internal investigations. This is simply my story and it rotates death, deception and degradation as fundamental and requisite experiences in a quest for understanding and growth.

I learned that my father's cut and dried world is not reality. My actions always resulted in sharp punishment. But my childhood indiscretions were never in question. That is, my father did not have to manufacture accusations in order to levy punishment. Also, my father did not allow me to wallow in the mud of corporal punishment to the point where self confidence would become non-existent. He always built me back up. He always wanted me to be productive.

How my father raised me had a profound effect on how I reacted to DEA management. What I came to realize was that by reacting, I was already at a huge disadvantage. Also, my father's world, while I still believe it to be relevant and righteous, has no link to the world of bureaucracies and politics. I found myself lost standing steadfast while surrounded by people with no principle except to move up the ladder by any means.

It was an exhaustive effort to write this story. It was painful to recall my father's death. Also, it was distressing to remember the isolation connected with being lied about, lied to and eventually removed from a "good" job. I had to separate my trials into two stories. The first of which lays the foundation for the ability to gain clarity for my situation.

Again, I do not profess to be a guru of any sort. I do not believe my experience to be any more difficult than yours during your bleak and depressing moments. Many of my reactions are a result of my world, or rather the world my father created for me, coming into direct conflict with the real world. People do what they must to survive. I did what I had to do. Thanks to my father for my "unconquerable soul."

CHAPTER 1

/.V.\

THREE WEEKS AFTER BEING FIRED, (I never looked at it that way), I sat on my favorite sofa looking straight through the television that hosted the 10:00 a.m. Sportscenter. In my lap were several Thrift Savings Plan statements. I finished looking at them. I had $67,000.00 in the account. I would have to make deductions. I battled that despair by focusing on the television previously ignored and realized that my favorite team, the Oakland Raiders, had made it to the AFC championship game against the Baltimore Ravens.

In between game analysis and hype, I returned to my original, solemn practice of thinking forward and looking back. The mortgage is due, we can't take the kids out of private school and I still have to pay the car note, I thought. Why didn't I just take the suspension? Because I did nothing wrong. What difference does it make, I would be employed. But I would have been miserable being owned by those people and knowing that termination would be but a minor mistake away. But I have two kids that depend on me. I also have a wife.

Thoughts like these vexed my mind leaving tasks undone and calls unreturned. I did not want to venture outside because I believed my neighbors knew I had been fired.

/.V.\

The family room had become my sanctuary the couch my pew and my thoughts, those conflicting, tormenting, discouraging thoughts, my lord.

The phone rang often during the day. I was sure it was well wishers wanting to express sympathy for recent events. I was already enamored in self-pity so compassion was not welcomed. The "why me" had not yet subsided to "why not me." I was ashamed and embarrassed so deeply that my little girls could not raise my spirits. I cried and laughed simultaneously unable to move the mountain of perplexity. Alone, I fell into a great depression.

I answered the phone this time hoping it was a telephone marketer that I could rip into. I needed an outlet this morning. My thoughts sank beyond despair. I could not find solace in taking the stance I had against the agency.

"Yeah", I answered the phone sharply.

It was my father. The voice of experience and a man that personified sacrifice for family. With all his knowledge and love, I could not candidly speak with him. I felt I had forfeited my family's financial future in a selfish, stubborn attempt to let the established, bureaucracy know that I was not going to compromise what I believed to be right for any job. I felt that my father would have taken the suspension so he could keep his job. Not because he believed that he was wrong but for his family. I believed my father would say he was wrong to keep his family and his plans for his children intact. Pondering those thoughts, I felt completely insignificant and merit less. That is why I could not openly communicate with him.

"Hey, man. What's up?" he asked.

"I ain't doin' nothin'. Just sitting here trying to figure out what chance the Raiders have against the Ravens." My voice swelled from being downtrodden to becoming full of the excitement that accompanies an anticipated sporting event.

"None."

"Don't think so, huh?" That was normally the time for a monetary wager. I thought better of it however.

"How you doin' today?" He asked with a hint of parental concern.

"Hanging in there, Pop."

I rose from the couch with significant effort. I sighed hard which indicated to my father that I just maneuvered from a very comfortable position.

"Were you sleep, boy?"

"Naw, Pop. I was just sitting here thinking about my next move."

"What did you come up with?"

That was his test of how well he taught me to deal with adversity. He waited to hear that I had risen from the bowels of misfortune and was able to plan for the future, in spite of my present situation. He wanted to hear that I was focused on the task at hand. What he heard was me going to the freezer and putting ice in a glass cup. I have a rule: do not drink before noon. I broke that rule about a week ago, right after it happened. My father knew I had turned to the bottle. I was sure my wife inundated him with pleas for help. I was sure he received those phone calls. I was sure he could relate to my situation for he had been there.

"Well, boy. What did you come up with?"

I was hoping that he could not hear the morning libation entering the glass. I am sure he did. The ice cracked exceptionally loud.

"I don't know, Pop." A hard swallow followed my comment.

"We need to hook up for breakfast. What you doing tomorrow?"

He knew I had nothing to do. I could not say no. I wanted to say no because his plans would interrupt my appointment with apathetic contemplation.

"Yeah, Pop. I'm open. I have nothing else to do."

"Just because you have nothing to do doesn't mean you can't do something."

My father always puzzled me with short lines that had an enormous amount of meaning. My favorite has always been 'If I tell you a mosquito can pull a plow, don't ask me how just hitch him up'. What he meant by his most recent expression was an enigma because I did not know what "something" to do.

"You know what Pop, let's meet at Home Cookin' tomorrow at 10:30. I have to take the girls to school first."

"Meet you there."

"Later, Pop."

When I hung up the phone, I knew I would have to tell him the whole story. That 'They don't want a black man challenging them' would not suffice. He would want to know what really happened. He listened intently to my complaints subsequent to my termination but did not fully understand why certain events transpired in the manner in which they did. Unfortunately, I did not know the entire truth. I had to manufacture an explanation before tomorrow.

Before getting my kids from school, I spent the day watching the television and trying to avoid reality. The blinds were completely closed and that provided superb atmosphere for my grief. Darkness held firm the family room and made it a place where hope and despair could coexist without being recognized. In the light, hope and despair cleaved my body like a guillotine. My face would show promise while every vital sign, every feeling and every movement was abdicated. I felt transparent and I probably was.

Picking my oldest daughter up from school was an arduous

trial. I had to wash the tear tracks from my face. I had to come outside of myself long enough to speak to the stay-at-home moms who were bewildered at my presence. I had to smile for my daughter, the one who knew me as a "Special Agent" without letting her know I was unemployed. I also had to pick up my baby girl who was in day care and meet the puzzled stares and inquiries with "shift change" lies and a confident mask only to return to the car and sink into the driver's seat with a heavy sigh of frustration I hoped my children did not notice. The car radio's volume was raised anytime a song was played that incited my children to clap their hands. I wished their happiness could be transferred to me; their genuine smiles and laughs, those which had eluded me for almost three years, I wanted to absorb. I could only watch them in the rearview mirror and be miserably amazed at their glee.

Dinner would normally be done when Michele came home. She shared my frustration but not my agony. She was supportive and very instrumental in my firm stance against the agency. When my steadfastness faltered and I began to fall victim to the agency's negative propaganda, she was there to tell me to stand strong and firm. She remained with me through drunken stupors and violent shifts in character. Michele was the stable force in my life that I wanted to distance myself from. I wanted everything to be chaotic, melancholy and vague. I wanted Michele's gleam to dim slightly. Not because I did not want her to succeed, but because I did not want the spotlight on my shortcomings. She had been with Philadelphia's City Solicitors Office for almost five years and had cultivated an impeccable reputation. She was thorough and well liked. Her skills as an attorney were not in question. Her appearance was striking and her personality made her more beautiful. I had become unsure of myself. Her confidence and my lack thereof were direct antipodes that beckoned

Λ/Λ

distance to intervene. Children made distance an impossibility. I carelessly cultivated seeds of frustration in Michele that bore fruit. Her routine became a smile and kiss to the kids, changing of her clothes, eating of dinner, bathing and putting the kids to bed, then telephone conversations that lasted for hours. We barely spoke nor did we want to see each other.

At breakfast, my father seemed fatigued. He yawned frequently.

"Man, I've been real tired lately."

I did not want to hear his problems. I was unemployed. He was retired, with a pension. In spite of my reluctance, I began to inquire as to the source of his weariness, believing that another's problem would help me forget about mine.

"You been partying?"

"Naw. I don't even go to church that often."

My father was not a man that exhibited his belief in Christ through his attendance at church on Sunday. I recall seeing my father in church on one occasion: when my grandfather died. When he said church, he meant a bar or a speakeasy where all the old heads hung to exaggerate their worth to the world through stories of what used to be.

"What!" I said in an astonished tone. "You're that tired?"

"Yeah, man. Yesterday, I did not get out of bed until one in the afternoon."

His confession caused me to internally ponder my waking pattern. On many days, had it not been for my daughters, I would have remained confined to my bed because I wanted to. My father did not want to be in bed. He loved being in social settings and doing aerobics at the Y. Remaining in bed during the day was unlike him. And I barely noticed. I didn't even ask about the transfusions.

"The afternoon, huh. And you didn't hang out late?"

M

My father shook his head in a dissenting fashion while he poked out his bottom lip.

He picked the brightest seats in the restaurant. The sun shone immaculately through the window, revealing even the tiniest specks on the silverware. I sat with my back to the window, as had become customary, so I could see who came through the door. The sun stared at my father through the window and he stared back. I could see that the forty odd years of smoking had dressed the whites of his eyes with a yellow tint. He lifted his chin and glanced over his nose into my eyes.

"I talked to your wife yesterday." His eyes widened as his left eyebrow rose. He wanted a reaction.

"You probably talk to her more than I do", I said with a slight laugh. I already knew what I wanted to order, but I looked at the menu anyway.

"Man, she's a good girl that has your best interest at heart. Don't mess that up now."

I wanted to explode at him. I wanted to say 'Hey! I'm a hell of a guy and she is lucky to have me'. But I did not feel she was lucky to have me anymore. I did feel that she was manipulating my family into thinking that she was the best thing that happened to me. If we argued, I heard about it from my father. If there were issues with the kids, I heard about them from my father. She blamed everything on the "job situation." Since I was unable to manage my "job situation", I interpreted from my father that anything that went wrong in my house was my fault. Normally, I would not have gone to such extremes but I was feeling isolated.

"I'm not messing anything up, Pop. I'm just tired. It's been a lot of things that happened to me the past three years. I have dealt with them. She's been there, but she don't understand."

M

That was the introduction my father wanted. I tabled my problems and now the discussion would ensue.

"What is it that she don't understand?" He asked, folding his hands on the table. His head tilted to the right as if only his left ear was functioning. He leaned forward slightly.

"Well, Pop. It's like this. She thinks one way and I think another. Nothin' you can do about that."

My father sat back visibly astounded by what he heard.

"You would throw away your marriage over that?"

"What do you mean, throw away my marriage? I'm not throwing anything away."

I always found it difficult to discuss my parents' dysfunctional relationship with my father. I believed it was none of my business. Likewise, I now believed that he was overstepping sacred boundaries. I wanted to tell him that it was none of his business. But Michele made it his business by telling him. She disclosed information that should have remained in-house. She did not need sympathy. She had a job. She had not been fired. Yet the attention I directed toward myself decreased the amount of attention I gave her. She needed attention and I was absent.

"Y'all know what y'all going to order?" The waitress' words allowed me to think about what to say to my father. Maybe I would tell him to mind his business. Maybe I would tell him I am deeply depressed. Maybe I won't say anything. I'll just let him think what he wants.

"And you, honey. What will you have?" I had thought through my father's order, missing everything he recited from the menu.

"Let me get pork sausage and french toast and cheese eggs, scrambled hard."

"To drink."

"Large apple juice."

M

I had been coming to this place to eat since it opened last year. Near 71st and Ogontz in the Oak Lane section of Philadelphia, it became my place of choice for breakfast. The food reminded me of those places my father used to take me to eat in North Philadelphia near 22nd and Lehigh and 23rd and Allegheny. Home Cookin', however, had a much nicer atmosphere. The tables were always clean and we were able to actually have room to eat without bumping elbows with the person next to you. Strangely enough, I recall bumping elbows with a huge, heavily bearded man when I was ten at a place in North Philadelphia. If those places had names, there was no marquee that announced it. When we bumped, I remember his dark, hairy face looking down upon me. He had grits in his beard. He smiled slightly then attempted to give me more room by sliding to his right. I swore I heard the bar stool moan. At Home Cookin', that man would have had enough room to sit at the bar without bumping anyone. He also could have had a bright, clean atmosphere. Maybe he would have enjoyed his food more.

Eleven o'clock brought a shift in the sun that placed it almost directly above our heads; out of my father's eyes and off my back. His fatigue and true condition seemed to hide with the sun's shift. He would not be able to avoid direct light from the uncompromising sun.

CHAPTER II

/.\.\

IN THE SPRING OF 1997, I had established myself as a competent criminal investigator. Five years of conducting investigations undermanned and underappreciated, as had most of my black predecessors, strengthened my resolve and forced forward superior ingenuity. Prior to gaining five years drug law enforcement experience, I had survived three months in Quantico, VA: the DEA Academy.

Located on the marine base, Quantico, VA., the academy seemed more like boot camp for marines than the production of federal agents. The physical training was arduous yet I performed it with relative ease. I had just completed four years of college football and I was 22 years of age. My body adjusted to the myriad of exercises and drills designed to rid this Academy of potential agents. We would go on runs that seemed endless, up and down steep hills, through pothole laden roads. Every half mile or so, the instructor would have the class stop and perform push-ups, sit-ups or whatever seemed to provoke a glimmer of weakness from any member of the class. The instructors would watch the faces of the class and, if they believed they saw someone who appeared to dislike or have difficulty with a task, would assume a drill sergeant type posture near that BAT (Basic Agent Trainee) and bellow discouraging comments or give multiple commands that the BAT could not follow so as to punish the BAT with extra push-ups. I was that guy that always was punished. My face wore a youthful arrogance that betrayed my fear of the situation. On the first day at the academy, we had to introduce ourselves to the class and the full DEA training staff. I told them where I was from and why I wanted to be a federal agent. I also told them who was responsible for my interest (and ultimately who was responsible for my hiring) in becoming an agent. After the complete class presentation, an instructor addressed me in private.

"Don't ever tell anyone who your friends are in this agency." His face and tone were not urgent enough for me to take heed. He was also white, which in my mind significantly lessened his credibility. As I stood speechless raising a suspicious eyebrow at the instructor, I immediately thought back to comments that black agents made to me regarding what my demeanor should be at the Academy. These older, what I thought were more experienced blacks, made it clear that "they" did not want me at the academy. The question "Why?" never was proposed to these agents. By possessing credentials, they earned the right to inform and direct a 22-year-old potential agent. Their word was good enough for me. All of these black agents said, "Keep your mouth shut and your eyes open." But trying to adhere to such a doctrine, without the experience of having been subjected to the agency and its methods, was a difficult task. I was accustomed to addressing and dealing with problems as they arose. The ideology that was presented to me stressed avoidance. I could not elude attention, no matter how quiet I was. I was too tall and too full of expression.

A BAT (Basic Agent Trainee) could not receive weekend

leave until after the completion of four weeks in the academy. During those four weeks, BAT's horded themselves around individuals with whom they felt comfortable. Blacks went to blacks. Whites went to whites. Fortunately, our class had eight blacks in the class of 45 BAT's. A significant surprise for an agency notorious for having a dearth of minority representation. I was the youngest of the black BATs. My roommate was also black. Keith was from southern California, 35 and married to a white woman. His nipple was pierced. He also was a former Navy SEAL. I realized Keith could be trusted during a conversation we had after a week of sparse sleeping

"How old are you, man?"

"Twenty-Two" I said it with a pride that denoted the acknowledgment that very few entered the academy at that age.

"Be careful, man. Do everything they want you to do. They don't want you here."

Erick was another elder statesman. He was about 36 but from New York. He did not have any piercing, but he was a former cop with the Washington, D.C. police department. Erick was more familiar to me than Keith. Erick talked, walked and acted like a black man thoroughly immersed in city life. Not the site seeing, museum going aspect of that life, but the dining at the neighborhood hole-in-the-wall joint and feeling completely comfortable type brother. He did not mince words when telling me that my color, age and demeanor were going to be problems.

"What are you, twenty-five?'

"Naw, brah, twenty-two." I was able to forgo proper speech with Erick because his voice was raspy, raw and relaxing. It reminded me of the playground and the old heads drinking forties and smoking weed. My response goaded Erick's eyes to widen and his upper body to become upright. He looked at every other person sitting at the table as if saying, "We need to help this boy." Arrogance would not allow me to see what everyone else seemed to know.

There was one black male that was close to my age. Kerry was 27 and previously worked at Merion Prison. He was a southern boy that did not talk much but appeared to be constantly lost in thought. He too had played college football. He was short, maybe 5'9", about Keith's height. But his body was cut and rippled which made him appear to be taller. He also warned me that my age, color and demeanor would cause problems at the academy.

We all were subjected to some form of torment at the hands of the instructors. Kerry was thought stupid because of his southern draw and silence. Erick had an old injury to his hip from his 82nd Airborne days that instructors would not allow to limit his physical activity. Keith had a white wife. He tried to keep that fact private but could not. The problems they had brought temporary attention from the instructors. I had an "attitude problem", which brought a barrage of scrutiny from the staff.

After the first legal test, I asked permission to go to Charlotte, NC to attend a friend's wedding. My class coordinator, Tina Ohara, seemed receptive to the request. It was after the four week purgatory period and, to that point, I had completed all tasks assigned satisfactorily.

"I don't think that's a problem, Maurice. Where's the wedding again?" She asked with a very pleasant disposition. I perceived her as a non-threatening woman. She was maybe 5'4", very thin and moderately attractive. She was in charge of my class and her appearance was the sort that invoked relaxation, not respect.

"Charlotte. I'm coming back on Sunday." I said, trying to leave her office without further conversation.

"How you like it down here so far?"

"It's alright Ms. Ohara. Lot of running." The comment made Tina laugh and I smiled because of that.

"Now, you're from Philly, right?"

"Yes I am, Ms. Ohara. The Mount Airy section."

"Mount Airy! I'm from Chestnut Hill!"

I had to engage her in conversation now. Mount Airy is very close to Chestnut Hill but worlds apart. Chestnut Hill was a pristine, quaint area of Philadelphia where many affluent individuals resided so that they could say they were "Philadelphians" and not suburbanites. Mt. Airy was a middle-class area that fell victim to a heavy influx of lower class influence and residents. We had nothing in common other than our differing perceptions.

"You want to go back to Philly after you graduate?"

"Sure. If they let me. If not, I'll go wherever. So where did you go to school? I went to Central."

Ohara's eyes went downward towards various papers scattered on her desk. I knew then that I was acting to familiar with a superior.

"Sign here, Maurice." She presented me with a sheet of paper that acknowledged my departure and return date for the Charlotte trip. I signed the paper and left the room saying "bye" with my back toward her.

When I returned on Sunday, I found my room full of anxious allies.

"What's up fellows? What's happening?"

I laid down my bag of clothes feeling each eye on me.

"Hope you had a good time. Shit is on now."

"What you talkin' about 'E'?' The enjoyable time spent in Charlotte was time I wanted to preserve and summon when the academy became trying. Erick's words pushed every grain of pleasure from me. I stood, after dropping my luggage, perplexed and angry that my joy had been stolen. "What the fuck is y'all talkin' about?"

"Did you let them know that you were leaving for the weekend?" Keith asked.

"I let Tina know. Why?" I knew that I was the baby of the crew but the parental like questions incited a rebellion that was displayed in the tone of my statement.

"Did you let Andy know?" Erick asked. I felt like I was being interrogated. Kerry sat on the bed speechlessly observing my reaction. Andy (Andrew Diamond) was one of three class instructors. He was directly responsible for a group of BATs of which I was part. He evaluated us and held biweekly conferences to evaluate our progress as BATs. My first mistake had been made.

"For what? I let Tina know and that's that." Indignation propelled those words forward briskly and directly. My eyes pierced directly into Erick's, like he was the only one in the room. After a brief stare, because Erick had to let me know that he was not to be browbeaten; Erick shook his head in frustration and disappointment. I stood watching his reaction while becoming dizzy with ignorance.

"You have to follow the chain of command, Maurice. You have to first ask Andy, who will ask Tina and if Tina needs too ask anyone else, she will do so. Andy was asking where you were this weekend. We didn't let him know where you went, but you know Tina did. Don't give them shit to get you on. Do it by the numbers." Keith's words brought to light points I had not previously contemplated.

"We'll help you, but you have to help yourself", Kerry said with a pitch of concern that compelled self examination.

I circumvented chain of command and went directly to Tina. I cannot recall why I did not let Andy know I was going to Charlotte. Maybe the conversation I had with Tina put me at ease because of our common areas of familiarization. Maybe I just believed that Tina was in charge, which she was, and that her approval superseded all others. Maybe I had just been set up. My only allies forced that point home.

When Monday arrived, I went to class knowing that everyone knew I went over Andy's head. That could not go unpunished because DEA held sacred the chain of command. During class, Tina removed me from the group and asked me to follow her. I followed her to the office of the Assistant Agent in Charge of Training. I was visibly confused as to what was happening but I attempted to remain composed amongst the tension. I quickly scanned the walls of his office and observed plaques of commendation from his former post of duty, Columbia, S.C. He was sitting behind his desk when I entered the room, reading manuals and other agency directives. He was wearing bifocals which he promptly removed when I entered. I stood directly before him separated only by the desk. Tina took refuge in the corner of the office after she closed the door. Upon removing his glasses, I, without interference, encountered his eyes. They were deep and blue and blatantly disdainful towards what was before him. It was as if my presence was a catalyst that provoked a fiery rage in that man. His eyes glowed with hatred. He spoke.

"I hope you had a good time this past weekend. But you won't be here much longer if you don't get your act together!" His comments were thunderously barked. He also pointed his finger at me-a form of reprimand of which I did not approve. My anger at being punished in such a fashion swelled to the point where tears began to flow. I tried to look past him, but those blue eyes and the hatred worn by them captivated my attention. When he saw the tears, he began to pounce with the ferocity of an aggressive, starved predator.

M

"Are you sure you want to be here? We can get you out of here if you like. You need to score much better on tests and you need to change your attitude!"

His southern draw augmented my anger. It invoked images of harsh discrimination which I had previously never encountered. His tirade continued but I heard little. I used all my senses to control my tongue and all my focus to evaluate the extent of his rancor. I was able to notice a snigger over my left shoulder. I knew I was amongst enemies. I was led back to class by Tina. I could not halt the feeling of betrayal and I never intentionally addressed her again.

My second mistake was not being able to shoot well. I never had occasion to fire a gun before the academy. We were on the firing range four, five times a week and on each occasion fired approximately 500 rounds. The novelty of being able to legally possess a gun quickly evaporated when my fingers were repeatedly frostbitten during the frigid months of January and February. I recall the laborious task of reloading a Sig Sauer 9mm with frozen fingers and the electric jolt that its recoil transmitted through my body. What was a rite of passage was rapidly becoming a one way ticket home.

To satisfy the shooting requirement, a BAT must have 70 out of 100 rounds inside a bottle shaped target. Shots are fired from varying distances: 50, 25 15, 10, 7 and 5 yards. I did not qualify the first time. That meant I had to take remedial shooting lessons. I was not alone so the embarrassment was minimal. Remedial shooting took place at an inside range at the academy. The instructors were helpful and attentive and genuinely concerned with the progression of our firearm proficiency.

I failed to qualify the second time. The academy gives you three chances to qualify. Because I failed, I had to attend more remedial training. There were four BATs in the remedial class now: Erick, Kerry, Christine (white girl from Philly) and

M

myself. I had already completed 10 weeks at the academy. The academy lasted approximately 14 weeks. At the end of the 11th week, we had to "shoot for our jobs." I was never quite as humble and unsure as I was during that time. I prayed more and I talked to my father more. Then the day came. We placed 100 rounds in our magazines and pant pockets. I called upon all that was holy to help me. The course began from the 50 yard line. I took ten shot from that distance sure that I did not hit the target. Upon the command from the range director, we ran to the 25 yard line, used cover and fired 15 rounds. Midway between firing at the 25, I had to reload a magazine. As I reached in my pocket to get rounds, I looked over my shoulder and saw Andy, Tina and two other instructors behind me. Since the other shooters were to my right, I noticed that they only had one instructor behind them. I did not have time to determine why four instructors were behind me, not until I finished the first portion of the qualification course. I completed the first 100 rounds and was confident that the target represented a qualifying score. As I turned to get another 100 rounds (the course had to be shot twice), I purposely walked in between the instructors.

"Excuse me." I said smugly.

My focus was gone. I was now more concerned with the instructors than I was with my target. As we moved from the 50 yard mark to the 25 yard mark and then to the 15 yard mark, I saw that my second target was not as decorated with holes as my first. After my final shots from the five yard mark, Andy sprinted to my target, removed it from the stand and personally carried it back to the tower to be counted. We all waited for the results. Erick was visibly confident. Kerry was quietly optimistic. Christine and I were hopeful.

"Okay. I got the results." The range director went to Erick and shook his hand.

$$\wedge\!\wedge$$

"I shouldn't have been here anyway. I just had a bad day the second time." After that comment, Erick strolled into the class already in progress.

"Mr. Brooks. Good job", the range instructor said to Kerry with a smile. Kerry accepted the hand shake and entered the classroom.

The range instructor then directed his attention towards me.

"Mister Williamson. Congratulations! 76 and 70." I looked at the huge smile on the range instructor's face and almost reciprocated. Then I caught myself. They wanted you to fail. Why smile at them? I shook his hand. Tina was there.

"Congratulations, Maurice." The advantage to being 6'3" is that you can look over people who are short. I used that advantage, giving her a brisk, "Thank you" as I went into the classroom. When I entered the classroom, my roommate gave me a congratulatory handshake. I was gleaming with a cockiness that was almost permanently taken. I got it back. Christine never entered the classroom.

My "fuck all y'all" attitude was back in place. My test scores were fine. My PT was fine. I had qualified. There was nothing they could do to me now. Keith, Kerry, Erick and myself would travel to D.C. regularly after qualifying, making the final weeks at the academy enjoyable. I could not contain my excitement when graduation was but a day away. My mother, father, sisters, nieces and nephews were there. NFL Commissioner Paul Tagliabu presented us our credentials and the gold badge. The ceremony was short and I quickly left the base without once accepting congratulations from any of the white instructors, not a hand shake or a nod of approval. I surrounded myself with the support group that helped me make it through the academy. I met their families and they met mine. Fortunately, our families were staying at the same hotel so we caravanned to that location. When we were at the hotel, an open door policy on the rooms made for extensive conversation between folks that had little in common other than being black and related to the graduates. While leaving one room, I overheard a conversation between Keith and my father.

"He had it hard, Mr. Williamson. They were thinking of ways to throw him out."

"Well, I'm glad you helped him then." My father replied.

"He had to help himself and if he wasn't so stubborn, he would have quit. They wanted him bad and he didn't quit."

I walked back toward the room I just left, bursting with pride. I was not ecstatic because I survived the academy. I had just been awarded true acceptance and respect from someone who observed me on the frontline. Just like I earned that badge and gun, I earned Keith's and most certainly Kerry's and Erick's, deference. The older blacks that counseled me regarding the academy were right. They did not want me there. That sentiment was reinforced by my support network at the academy. I knew that if I was not wanted at the academy, I would not be welcomed in the field. I had proven myself to be comfortable wearing the swagger of a survivor. What I did not want to realize was that the people that conspired against me to have me falter in the academy had an extensive network in the field. Phone calls had been made. I had survived the academy. That academy was only 14 weeks. I had unlimited time to be a special agent and they would have unlimited opportunity to ruin my career.

M

CHAPTER III

/.\/.\

I WAS ASSIGNED TO THE PHILADELPHIA FIELD DIVISION. My hometown. A twenty-two year old man with a federal badge in his hometown. It was unusual for an agent to be assigned to the city where he was hired. However, the government decided that money was low and they would not transfer/ rotate agents as they normally would. I benefited from their lack of financial ability. They wanted to send me to Los Angles. I dodged that trip.

I loved to party and knew the spots to frequent to ensure a good time. I had a crew: my "boys" that I hung out with often. My main man was Ronnie. He was involved with things that I could no longer witness. Ronnie was my boy since junior high. His youthful involvement in the "neighborhood business" strengthened his reputation and influence throughout the neighborhood during high school and while I was away at college. He was a talented basketball player that had no time to perfect his ability. He was too busy perfecting other skills. I was constantly amazed at his propensity to obtain any item upon request. If you wanted a record player, he could get it. If you needed weed, he could get it. I recall having problems with a few neighborhood people while I

/.\/.\

lived at 5th and Q Streets, NW Washington, DC. The problems were not severe but I felt escalation of the problems would result in serious conflict. I had to be prepared. I was interning with the State Department during summer recess from college and knew no one in DC. I told Ronnie of the problems I was having and he sent me a semi automatic .45 caliber handgun via FedEx. The gun glistened when I opened the package. It was already loaded. I was scared to death because I never handled a gun and he did not send the operation manual. Luckily, I did not have to use the gun and it remained in the closet under towels. When I returned the gun to Ronnie, I remember him asking if everything was "straight."

I knew Ronnie had my back. His many connections and lack of "professional" aspiration never damaged our friendship. He encouraged my pursuit of education and supported my new professional law enforcement career. For his loyalty, I reciprocated with weekly interaction that involved the consumption of Canadian Mist and adult entertainment. A brand new federal agent in the "booty club" drunk as hell. Our deepest and most intimate conversations would occur in loud clubs with topless women gyrating and twisting.

"Dawg! How you like being a fed!" His smile was sincere and robust when he spoke. I had a young lady performing a table dance. She had her back to me, so she could not hear what Ronnie said.

"It's alright man. I'm just getting started. Not that many brothers in there, though."

"Dawg, you the only nigger up in there!" He almost seemed paternal.

"Naw, it's some older brothers up in there. But not many."

I dug in my pocket and gave the female a $10.00 bill. I resumed my drinking.

"Yo, dawg, what was it like down at that school? How

long were you down that place?" Ronnie and I did not have
to see each other or even speak to each other to be tight.

"Shiiiiit. I think I was there about 14 weeks. Fourteen
weeks of bullshit from them white boys. Know what I mean?
I mean, man, they ain't shit. They were trying to fuck me the
whole time I was there."

Ronnie just looked at me shaking his head in agreement.

"Oh, shit, look at that bitch! Look at that ass on that
motherfucker!" Ronnie's comments were appropriate and
timely. For a brief minute, I began to feel awkward because of
the professional distance between us. Another drink would
make less my feeling of duty. Two more drinks and life would
be like it was when I was 19, just four years ago.

The SAC (Special Agent in Charge) assigned me to a clan-
destine laboratory group. That group was charged with the
investigation of methamphetamine, dangerous and exotic
drugs like phencyclidine (PCP), LSD and ecstasy. The group's
major clientele were the motorcycle gang type that transported methamphetamine. The group was not conducive to
the success of black agents. There were two other blacks in the
group and they served a subservient role and no role, respec-
tively. The former was a black female named Bernadette. She
was married to a white male. She was thoroughly receptive to
the intrinsic military aspect of the agency. It was rare that she
questioned an order. It was rare that she relayed her ideals to
coworkers regarding investigations and how the job could be
enhanced. She went along to get along. She was almost thirty,
doing nothing and making good money. Charles was in his
mid-forties and from my perspective, waiting to retire. He
was a Vietnam veteran that had many stories about his days in
combat. He would openly use "gook" to describe the "slant
eyed bastards" that killed many of his friends. Charles seemed
content with his current station within the agency. He was a

13, which meant he was making almost 90k. Our first conversation was brief.

"They sent you to group one, huh." Charles had a high, happy voice that made me comfortable.

"Yeah. Maurice Williamson." I extended my hand and we shook.

"Who the hell did you piss off to get in here. They could use you more over the task force."

"I think I pissed off everybody!" I said with a wide smile.

"I can tell", Charles retorted returning the smile. "I heard about you at the academy. We didn't think you were going to make it. Glad you did, though"

"What, did y'all have a bet on me or something!" I said laughing. "It wasn't easy down there."

"It's never easy for us. It's not going to be easy for you here either."

"Maurice Williamson", the group secretary bellowed. "Mr. Roberts wants you in the front office."

"Thanks", I replied. As I rose from my desk, I nodded at Charles bidding him farewell.

"Oh yeah, brother. I almost forgot. Every brother ain't a brother." He said as his voice and face switched from mild to stern. I gave no visible response but thought about that comment and to whom that comment was directed on my way to the office of Lewis Roberts.

Lewis Roberts was the reason I was employed with DEA. He knew my mother through her community service endeavors and DEA's community outreach programs. He was a 39-year-old Assistant Special Agent in Charg e (ASAC) who began his career with DEA when he was twenty-two. In New York, he had killed a man during undercover negotiations. When I saw Mr. Roberts, I saw what I could be in the agency. He was a very young ASAC and his star was rising rapidly. He would be a

SAC within three years. Mr. Roberts was not homogenized, surprisingly. That is, he had a strong sense of service to our community and he did not speak as if his success in DEA alienated him from black folk. He was always at "black" functions. I felt I could trust him and that he had my best interest at heart. I aspired to be where he was.

"Maurice! Close the door. Grab a seat." Mr. Roberts had a sweet bass-like voice of confidence that beckoned obedience. Not like my father's, but close enough to conjure father like respect. "I've been swamped here and haven't had a chance to talk with you since you've been back from the academy. How's everything going?"

"Good Mr. Roberts. I'm getting situated and reading some of the cases in the group so I'll know what's going on."

"Good. Good idea, Maurice. A lot of guys wouldn't take the time to do that." While he was speaking, the warm smile that Mr. Roberts donned was erased by the unavoidable question. "What happened at the academy?" He asked. I recoiled with an enigmatic look. You know exactly what was going on down there, I thought. I was black and they did not want me to be an agent.

"You were sent there as a scholar. That means your test scores should have been in the nineties." Mr. Roberts paused and seemed to reflect on his experiences as an agent. He thought it better to build than to break. "You know what though, you're here now. You are an agent."

"Yeah, but I don't want you to feel like I let you down. I did the best I could under the circumstances."

"It doesn't matter, Maurice. The thing is you're here now. If you need help or have any questions, just ask me. Alright?"

"Okay, Mr. Roberts."

"You got any plans for lunch. Let's go get a bite."

That was the first of many times that Roberts and I went

to lunch over the course of three years. Other agents, white and black, began noticing that Roberts had an interest in my professional development. Roberts would openly proclaim that I had a "friend up front." Those who did not have a "friend up front" treated me suspiciously. Rank and file law enforcement people perceived interaction with superiors as "brown nosing." The person accused of such violation was destined to become an outcast. The sting of ostracism, by white and black agents, forced forward fierce denials that fell on deaf ears. I was alone because I had a rapport with Roberts. I was being taught a lesson. I asked a black agent that lived in my neighborhood to pick me up from the service station because the oil in the car needed to be changed. When he arrived at the station, I could see that he was not pleased with being there. The look of contempt and derision painted his face with deep wrinkles about his forehead and a bent mouth.

"What's going on, man. Appreciate you coming to get me."

"Yeah." His tone and inflection mirrored his facial demeanor. I was boiling with anger and incensed by the lethargic greeting.

"What is going on?" I asked, still unaware of the unwritten laws governing association.

"You know what's going on, don't you?"

"I don't know what the hell you're talking about."

"Well, back in slavery times, some black folks worked in the fields picking cotton. Other black folks worked in the house because they got friendly with mas'r. You know what those people were called?" When he asked the question, his eyes never left the road but, peripherally, he was looking for a physical response. What he received was an even more perplexed face than the one that met his contemptuous stare.

"They called them house niggers. And that's what you are. A house nigger. Meeting and greeting with the man so you don't have to do shit. We're all investigators here. We know what's going on. And you are a house nigger."

I turned to face the road and watched as the yellow lines passed. The thought of being called an "Uncle Tom" or a "House Nigger," losing the acceptance of individuals that I depended upon, launched tears that were unsuccessfully delayed. I was exposed not for being a "house nigger" but for being pushed to tears by false accusations. That made me worker harder and alone.

During the next four years, I was the case agent for investigations that led to the arrest and conviction of legendary narcotic manufacturers and distributors. During that time, Roberts left to become SAC in Detroit. Rank and file people, especially the black agents, welcomed me back in the fold after his departure. They believed I was like them now, exposed and vulnerable to the wavering edict of divisional management.

Since moving out the house some four years earlier, my father and I talked more often. I commuted from South Jersey to West Oak Lane and coached little league football with my father. My father was, appropriately, the head coach. He was 5'11", 220 pounds and beyond black. His deep baritone voice barked orders to kids and coaches alike. No one publicly questioned him because his stature coupled with his intonation forced immediate compliance. Talk of games and teaching the kids how to play football served as the catalyst to begin a more in depth conversation. The crux of our dialogue revolved around my survival in the "white man's world." My father often teased that he was once as stubborn as I; not able to finesse his way through the vicarious and ubiquitous stratagems white people would employ. During one of our many conversation that calculated the football worth of a juvenile participant, my father flowed into a discussion regarding my novice interpretation of the "real world."

"How you like the job, man? Havin' fun yet?"

"Yeah, yeah, Pop. It's cool."

"Everything goin' alright?"

"I already told you everything was cool, Pop." I often became irritable at multiple inquiries. I always felt the person was looking for more than they were willing to ask. This was the case with my father's query.

"Maurice, I've known you longer than you've known yourself."

I was also known for internalizing thoughts and problems. I would ponder events and occurrences and stay silent, unless asked. If asked, I had the gift of unabashed honesty which was not much a blessing when dealing with deceitful people. That is what law enforcement and the agency are all about: deceit. They try to shape and mold events so as to fit the version they want believed. What actually happened never appears. However, the presentation of the investigative events would be so full of conviction and supporting data, no one would ever question the facts. I was having problems adjusting to the game on that field. I was used to things being the way they appeared. I tried to keep life simple. That was a dangerous doctrine to hold in a law enforcement environment. It conflicted directly with the credo of the overwhelming majority who had graduated from DEA's school of deception. A common and well deserved take on DEA's name is "Deception at Every Angle." I did not subscribe to common perspective. I believed that if a person was a drug dealer, it would show and creation of facts and scenarios was a useless consumption of time.

"I know, Pop. But you know how those white folks are. If you don't roll with them, they try to roll over you. I can't go for that. I know just as much if not more than them. I know what a real drug dealer looks like and acts like. They go after fleas and act like they made the biggest case ever. What's sick about it, the supervisors give them awards like they really did something. I just don't get it."

My father laughed slightly while displaying a smirk of wisdom.

"Welcome to the real world, boy!" He addressed me with a sympathetic yet thankful tone. My father rose from his lazy boy recliner and went to his fully stocked wet bar.

"Want a drink?"

"What you got over there? Not that Wild Turkey."

"Yeah. I got some of that. Want some?"

"Why not. It's Saturday. Mix it with some coke. Please!"

On that day and night, my father and I consumed a bottle of Wild Turkey. We figured out the problems of the world and how they should be solved. He determined who I should marry and when I should have kids. I did not resolve much that night regarding the quandary at work. I did learn that it is easier to converse with fathers when you move out and have your own house, car and bills. I also knew I had a supporter that had experienced discrimination.

I dated many women. I had one long term relationship that was ultimately destroyed by my fierce desire to be with more than "the girl at home." When she left, I had an abundance of freedom and options. I took full advantage of both. When I met Michele, my future wife, there were absolutely no plans for a child or anything more than a casual relationship. She was an attorney struggling to pass the bar exam. I provided her with frequent free meals, room and board and the opportunity to study in peace. She uplifted my mind with her intelligence and insight, offering much more than the women I was accustomed to dating. Before I fell completely, she was pregnant. I would now have two souls to take care of. Strangely, I was excited about the prospect of losing the freedom that comes with child rearing.

The birth of my first child, Jordyn, provided my father with great joy and pride. We both wanted a boy, but figured that she could play sports also. When he arrived at the hospital, he had flowers for my future wife, Michele, and balloons and stuffed animals and all the other things that first time grandparents buy to welcome a new grandchild. We barely talked that day, just exchanged smiles and nods.

I was on trial when Jordyn was born. I had arrested five defendants during the course of an investigation and no one pled. I traveled from court to the hospital and spent three nights on an extremely uncomfortable cot that I blame for my lower back problems. I remember that pride prevented me from returning home and encouraged my staying with Michele and Jordyn. Prior to Jordyn's birth, Ronnie helped me prepare the baby's room by offering his services to paint. We drank most of the time but ultimately did complete the task. I asked him how everyone was doing. I had been busy at work and home and unable to participate in our weekly outings for about eight months. I was apologetic but Ronnie would not hear it.

"I been busy as hell at work. The only thing I do now is come home, eat and sleep."

"Nigger, you doin' more than that or I wouldn't be here painting!" His retort was the catalyst for a heartfelt laugh that I missed. Ronnie was genuine. He did not want anything from me nor I from him. We just enjoyed the honesty and comfort our interaction paraded. I did not experience the discomfort of wearing false smiles or speaking deceitful words. I could just relax with Ronnie because he was from around the way. But Ronnie was a convicted felon. He was arrested when during my junior year of college and served some time.

Federal agents are not allowed to associate with known felons. I had one in my house. The consequences of doing what I knew to be right were temporarily subdued by unfeigned conversation. My fraternity brothers were all in Carolina and he was the only person from Philly that I trusted. I was not in to making new friends because there is always secretive baggage that accompanies those acquaintances. Besides, I had no desire to reveal my line of work to people I just met.

"You know black Ant got locked up for murder." Ronnie always provided information about the old crew. I realized I was being tested to see where my allegiances were.

"Naw, what happened?" That was the right answer. I had to show concern that validated acknowledgment of my roots.

"He was doing something for me and the motherfucker tried to rob him. Ant knocked the gun out the boy's hand and pulled his shit on him. Shot that motherfucker three times."

I stopped painting and placed a grave stare in Ronnie's direction. He seemed not to notice and continued painting.

"I really don't need to know all that shit, know what I'm saying?"

"Oh yeah, that's right. You the man. I just wanted you to know what was happening around the way."

"Thanks, but I'll read the paper."

"You didn't read about it?"

"No, didn't see it. How's moms doin'?" I asked, changing the topic of conversation.

"She's doin' good. She just came back from A.C. She didn't win shit but she had a good time. She asked about you the other day. I told her you're having a baby. She says you better bring that baby over for her to see when it's born or else!" Ronnie smiled and we forgot about mutual acquaintances from the neighborhood. We focused on our upbringing and the many beatings we received from our parents. Our parents were interchangeable. That is, if I was at his house, Ronnie's mother and father became mine and vice versa. Unfortunately, bad behavior and childhood indiscretion did not remain at just one house. Thus, heavy discipline was levied at both residences. We were able to reminisce fondly about the leather belt beatings we received as youngsters. Blame circulated freely from Ronnie to me and back as we determined who was at fault for many of the beatings. Ultimately, I admitted that I was punishment's origin. He agreed. And I became an agent, Ronnie a criminal. I marveled at the differing result of like discipline and upbringing.

When the baby came home, I had just completed the jury trial that resulted in the conviction of three longtime methamphetamine manufacturers and distributors. I took the week off to bask in the glory of a new child and a successful conclusion to a lengthy investigation. When I returned to work, my pride at producing a daughter and arresting several career criminals created a haughty exterior that broadcast what I felt: I am better than y'all and I can prove it! I did prove it. No one my age and with the same years of experience could have handled the investigations I spearheaded. Many of my white contemporaries were being nurtured by supervisors. They were being fed investigations much like a mother bird feeds her chicks. There was little to be done in these cases but to testify as to what another had already done. Somehow, those cases were praised and awards were given to those "case agents." I was never given anything. To broaden the statement, blacks were not given anything. If a black agent were given a case, I am sure he or she would feel anachronous. It is the norm in DEA and every other federal agency that black agents have to take mustard seed sized investigations and construct complex criminal conspiracies with limited resources. I do not wish to state that identical resources are not available

M

to blacks that are to whites, but it is extraordinary how resources suddenly shrink, both manpower and fiscal, when the case agents are black. I was beyond that. I had made a mark and would not settle for anything less.

/.\.\

CHAPTER IV

∕.∖.∖

A YEAR AFTER JORDYN'S BIRTH, Michele and I were married. She had since passed the bar and was working in the City Solicitor's office. She was having no problems at work nor was I. I gained the support of my group and my supervisor Gary.

I received a call while I was the duty agent. The duty agent has to answer the seemingly endless calls from citizens that proclaim to have knowledge of drug activity. Very few are credible and many are repeat callers grabbing much needed attention. I did not like being the duty agent, especially on the weekends. But this call captured my attention. The caller was obviously white. He said his name was Michael Friend.

"Yes. I'd like to give some information." Friend said.

"What type of information", I replied while placing the log book in front of me. "What's your name first off?"

"Do you really need my name to take the information?"

"Look man, I don't have time for this. Do you have a name or not?"

"Well, what's your name?"

"None of your goddamned business. You called here. If you have some information, the way we start is by getting your name."

∕.∖.∖

"Michael's my name", he said in a defeated voice.

"Okay, Michael, what you got for me?"

"I know these guys who move a lot of weight. A lot."

"A lot of weight of what? Coke, smack, weed?"

"They move everything. I mean everything. You name it, they got it. I ain't bullshittin'." The way he spoke was quick, as if he just finished using speed.

"Who are these guys?"

"Black guys. I think they're hooked up with the junior black mafia. They know a lot of people who are in the junior black mafia." By now, the JBM (Junior Black Mafia) had been dismantled and its members had been jailed or killed. Maybe they're trying to start up again, I thought.

"Alright, Mike. How about you come in and see me and we can discuss this more."

"I don't know, man."

That was the response that indicated either lack of veracity or fear. Either way, it was less paper for me to push if he declined to come in. I still had to coax him to provide information.

"Well if you don't come in, there's nothing I can do."

"When do you want me to come in?" He said in that increasingly familiar defeated voice.

"You know where the federal building is? We're on the 10th floor. Come to the office tomorrow at eleven. We'll talk more then. Cool?"

"Yeah. Tomorrow at eleven. Okay. See you then."

Tomorrow inevitably arrived and Mike was at DEA's Philadelphia office at 10:45. I was impressed and intrigued. A call-in source of information that expressed reluctance to speak with me in person arrived before the scheduled time. I was sitting at my desk delaying the start of a task that was not investigation related. My phone rang and the receptionist alerted me to Michael's presence.

"Hey, Jimmy. Got a second?" I was assigned to a task force. A task force is comprised of various federal, state and local law enforcement officers on loan to DEA so that all resources are available for narcotics investigation. I teamed with Jimmy, who was from Secret Service, and made sure he did DEA's paperwork correctly. My role as advisor fostered a friendship between us. Whatever he wanted to do, I supported. He did likewise.

"Yeah, what's up?" he said, closing his newspaper.

"I got a snitch up front and I need somebody to sit in on the interview. Should only take about half hour."

"Let's go."

We walked to the reception area talking about kids, he had two and I one. I told Jimmy to prepare an interview room and I would bring the snitch there. When I opened the door to the reception area, I saw a white male sitting. He wore glasses and was at first glance awkward. He stood when he saw my head lean through the door's opening. When he stood, I noticed that he was a frail but tall man with a nose that disclosed his Jewish lineage. As he walked toward the door, the receptionist seemed amazed by his thinness. Hell, this guy has AIDs, I thought.

"Michael?" I asked, wanting to make sure it was the same person I spoke to the day before.

"Yes. Maurice, right." He answered extending his hand.

"Yeah, Special Agent Maurice Williamson." I wanted to establish parameters early. If his information was credible and I had to utilize him to make buys and obtain information, he had to know that I was in charge. I did not want him to feel comfortable initially because the interrogation would be sharp and direct. His handshake mirrored his physical appearance and exposed his weakness. My job was to determine why a weak person would want to involve himself in the drug game.

We arrived at the interview room and I introduced him to Jimmy in an official manner. I sat Michael against the wall away from the desk. I wanted his every move visible and thus scrutinized. The interview began with Michael repeating what he told me over the phone. After 1/2 an hour of question and answer, I made the tough inquiry.

"So why are you doing this, Michael."

"Call me Mike, please", he said pleading for informality.

"Not a problem. Now answer the question."

"Well it's like this, Maurice. I have a car dealership that you can use and you can wire it up and put cameras in and see that I am telling the truth about these guys. I'm telling you they're big time."

"Why you want to give them up then?" I asked.

"I want to get out of here and start all over. I got mixed up in some things before and I just want to start again." he said looking me sternly in the eye. I turned my head toward Jimmy and caught his eye. He thought Mike was full of shit also.

"So you've been arrested before?" Jimmy asked after a brief moment to ponder Mike's excuse for wanting to snitch.

"Yes I have."

"How many times?" Jimmy rapidly responded.

"Four maybe five times. But they all were bull. This guy, Steven Wesson, has a hard on for me."

"Who is Steven Wesson?" I said motioning for Mike to slow down while my note taking became current with the conversation.

"You ready, Maurice?" Mike asked containing his speech temporarily.

"Go head." I said.

"Okay. Wesson is this guy that works as an investigator

/\/\

with New Jersey. He's been after me for years ever since I brought my dealership over there. He doesn't like my clientele, you know what I mean?" Mike looked directly at me as if I understood. I could not tell him that I did.

"No. What do you mean?"

"I mean those people do not like blacks. So he fucks with them by fucking with me."

"All your clients from Philly?"

"Most are."

"Okay, Mike. I have to check out what you're telling me. I also have to check you out. It will take a few days and then we'll see what happens. Alright?" I asked waiting to see a reaction.

"No problem." he responded.

We walked Mike to the elevator and bid him farewell. As soon as the door closed, Ron and I looked at each other and exhaled. We began processing Mike as a confidential informant. During that process, we found that he had been arrested five times; four were felony arrest. Mike had been arrested for fraud and deception of customers. That clarified his status as a liar, but all snitches lie. It becomes a control issue. Will I be able to believe this guy and will he follow my directions, I thought. DEA has an adage: You can't expect a dove to mingle with the rats. If you want a rat, you have to send a rat. We had a very good rat. The question now was could I offer more cheese than the other side.

The couple of days it normally took to establish an informant took several weeks for Mike. Mike was on probation in Pennsylvania so I had to call his probation officer there and get special permission to use him as a DEA informant. I had to thoroughly outline the advantages of using this informant to my superiors, which included the new SAC, Barry Sweeney. Only the SAC could approve the use of an informant with abundant felonies. Ultimately, SAC Sweeney did approve the use of Mike as a snitch.

The first job transpired on South Street at a Tattoo Parlor. Mike met with a guy named Jerome and purchased two ounces of cocaine. We normally dealt with significantly more weight of narcotics so we expected the transaction to occur quickly. It did not. Mike was wired and he talked with Jerome for almost an hour. Nothing was wrong, Mike just enjoyed talking. Then Jerome had to take a trip to where the drugs were. Despite being told not to front the money, Mike gave Jerome the money before he received the drugs. Jimmy and I were in the car profanely proclaiming Mike as a misfit. Fortunately, Jerome went to the drug house which was identified by other agents and returned. No money lost and no one knew it had been fronted. After the deal, Jimmy and I took a statement from Mike at which time we reiterated that he is never to front the money again.

"I'm sorry, Maurice. It'll never happen again. Listen, what you really need to do is wire up my store. They talk to me.", he said.

Mike's first deal, while not flawless, resulted in the identification of a drug house and a new player. The worse that could happen is a search warrant for the house and an arrest warrant for Jerome. The small step had been taken. Jimmy and I agreed. Maybe Mike is okay. If nothing happens, we can take the camera down.

So we did. We placed a closed circuit television in his office that also recorded sound. Over the next six months, I observed an extensive group of black males divulge secrets of the trade. They discussed where they picked up, stashed and distributed narcotics in detail. They discussed murders, corrupt cops and international connections. The scope of the investigation was huge. The group, as was I, was amazed at the candor with which this group discussed their operations with Mike. We purchased guns, drugs and were able to obtain the major money laundering mechanism utilized by this organization. The investigation was going well. Suddenly, I was transferred to the background investigations group which meant I had to investigate potential special agents to ensure their suitability to become criminal investigators. Gary, the supervisor that provided me support, was transferred to headquarters. At another juncture in my career, I may have believed that responsibility to be vital and of great importance. However, I knew better. It was well known that the background investigations group was the brain child of the administrator and that those without major investigations or without "friends up front" would be assigned. Despite having a premier case, I had no friends. Roberts's departure left me without a friendly hand with influence and my "my house is paid for" persona rendered me a threat and misunderstood by divisional management and their special agent snitches.

I was not going to allow Barry Sweeney, the SAC of Philadelphia's field office, to ruin this investigation. I worked hard to obtain multi-agency assistance and had ensured that charges related to their areas of expertise were incorporated into my investigation. That is, every agency had something to gain from this investigation. The IRS had tax evasion, the ATF had guns and there was counterfeiting involved so even the Secret Service would be happy. Sweeney's slight forced me to consider why such an action was necessary. He usurped the Administrator's directive that required only senior GS-13 be assigned to the background investigations to ensure that I had a place in that group. I was a GS-12. I was not yet eligible to be considered for promotion to a GS-13. This case, I was sure, would propel me to the GS-13 level. I relayed my sentiments to a John Buchanan. He was on loan from the Philadelphia's district attorney's office and a long time law enforcement veteran. He was also black. I envied the way he was able to maneuver in circles where I was not welcomed or did not wish to fraternize. He had the ability to make everyone feel intrinsic self worth by the manner with which he interacted. He was steady and stern and never hastily made accusations or decisions. John was a thinker, a thinker that posed no threat yet relayed threatening thoughts in a cerebral manner that only those listening intently could comprehend. I listened to John. His experience and his demeanor captured and held my admiration. Emulation was an impossible task, however. I recall speaking to John about my impending transfer.

"They don't like to see a young black male that knows what he is doing actually do it", he said. "You should be doing undercover and the such. Not being the case agent on a case like the one you have. The case has everything. You have drugs, guns, murders, money laundering. Hell, you have everything DEA should want in an investigation and they don't want you, the person with the most knowledge about the case, to do it. They're shooting for you." He spoke in such a matter of fact way that it appeared that he was questioning my skills of observation and why I had not arrived at the same conclusion.

Shortly after joining the background investigations team, I was assigned the background of Craig Schwartz. The background investigation was relatively simple. Schwartz had only two jobs and they were in the same area. While in college, however, Schwartz was arrested for making and possessing false identification (driver's license) for the purchase of alcohol while under aged. Schwartz pled guilty and performed community service. I viewed Schwartz's transgression as serious enough to disqualify him from employment consideration with DEA. I cited the "intentional and deliberate falsification of official documents" as the major factor for denial in my formal report. Two days later, I was summoned to the office of Barry

Sweeney. He wanted to know why Schwartz had not been recommended. When I sat, I felt the heat of trepidation engross my body. Sweeney peered at me from behind his desk and over his bifocals. When his head returned to an upright position, he removed his glasses as if he were preoccupied with other matters.

"What's this thing, Maurice, this thing with Scwartz?" He raised his arms, placed his hands behind his head and sat back in his chair. He was perplexed.

"What do you mean, sir?" I said grabbing hold of the chair's arms. Sweeney leaned forward and interlocked his fingers as if praying I would gain comprehension without him uttering words.

"This Schwartz thing. Why didn't you recommend him?"

"Because he intentional falsified documents, sir. It's in my report."

"Yes, I see that. But you know what, I know a lot of guys on this job who have done worse. I think maybe you should further justify your position." Sweeney's eyes grew grave and intense. I remember thinking that falsification is enough.

"Is there anything else that you found during your investigation?" Sweeney asked.

"Well, no sir." He then handed me the investigative file.

"Let's see if you can articulate your position a little more. I'm not saying change your recommendation, but I think you owe it to Mr. Schwartz to allow for college mistakes." He nodded his head up and down in a mocking fashion as if saying 'You know what I want done. Just do it.'

While returning to the group, my mind scurried with rebellious thoughts. When I arrived to the group, I was greeted by Fred. Fred was the new supervisor of the task force. He replaced Gary. Fred came from the Newark Field Office and served under Sweeney, when Sweeney was an Assistant Special Agent in Charge. The higher you go, the tighter the circle. Fred's face wore a rare and infrequent smile that denoted pleasure from someone's misery. He approached my desk and spoke.

"What was that all about?" Fred asked. Fred already knew what happened. He and Sweeney were friends and had already discussed my report.

"Oh, nothing. Just this background shit."

"He wanted you to change your recommendation, huh?" Fred's smile seemed to broaden as I marveled at his reckless-ness at not advising me that a background I conducted was being scrutinized.

"Maybe."

"Life's choices. You have your pay check in one hand and your principals in another. I guess the paycheck won."

I did not respond. I just watched as the slovenly man meandered toward his office and out of sight. Fred was right. I did change my recommendation from nay to aye in favor of Mr. Schwartz. Afterward, I felt like a whore that, even by whorish standards, had been mistreated and violated repeat-edly by unwelcome entry. I felt I had breeched the rules my father established for true manhood. I was swayed by the powerful and submitted to what I believed was wrong.

Fred was a large, slovenly person and lazy acting supervisor that baited all his subordinates with his lethargic approach to proactive law enforcement. If an employee acted as he, Fred would immediately discuss that employee with Sweeney in a negative fashion. Fred was responsible for the transfer and removal of five other task force members. My circumstance was different. I had already discerned that Fred was "stupid like a fox." So I made him work. If I had to conduct background investigations and continue criminal investigations, he would have to be active. That kept Fred busier than he wished to be because a supervisor must be present when the group hit the streets. The numerous jobs I would schedule along with other group members kept him moving. I never wanted him there for my jobs so I would articulate reasons why his presence in the office would serve the group's overall mission. Fred started to realize that I did not respect his prowess as an "effective" and "knowledgeable" agent. However, he never approached or questioned me. Fred's laziness was not my only concern. He jeopardized my life and the lives of at least six other agents because of his lack of decision making.

A member of our group wanted to purchase a kilogram of cocaine from a drug dealer that had sold that member sham narcotics. Sham narcotics are drugs that are not really what they purport to be. The group member previously purchased ½ ounce of heroin from this defendant. A field drug test indicated that he had purchased junk. When the "drugs" were sent to the laboratory for analysis, I am sure that the lab technician laughed. Under ordinary circumstances, the group would have arrested the defendant. Fred decided against it. Shortly after discovering he purchased junk, the group member received a call from the defendant asking if he wanted to purchase a kilogram of cocaine. Fred's interest in the case was resuscitated. Fred futilely assumed the posture of seasoned supervisor. When a Lieutenant from the Philadelphia Police department grabbed control of setting logistics for the operation, Fred reverted to his normal laissez-faire self.

Lt. Tony Newsome made plans in our group as to how the undercover deal should transpire. What was absent from Lt. Newsome's planning was the case's prior history. Had he known that the group member had purchased sham narcotics, the deal would have been canceled. At this time, the undercover is broadcasting that I have money and I'm stupid: a combination ripe for a rip. Fred never supplied that information to the lieutenant. I could not watch a job that initiated in our group be planned without our input. I began to direct the team as to locations where the deal should occur and appropriate language to use during negotiations. I also suggested that another undercover accompany our team member during the deal. Lt. Newsome liked the idea. He assigned one of his guys to go. Fred sat motionless in a chair. His stare fixed upon me when I made the suggestion. My stare was directed towards Lt. Newsome, as were my ideas and respect. Fred became a spectator; a $106, 000 dollar a year spectator. I realized that expertise in criminal investigations was not a factor when he became a supervisor. His survival skills relied on office politics and work repression. He somehow manipulated his way to a supervisory position by doing the least amount of work and remaining obedient. In an instant, our group's focus was on Lt. Newsome. Fred's disappointed and despondent eyes could not be concealed by his glasses as the briefing concluded.

The deal was to take place at McDonald's at 40th and Walnut. The location had easily accessible exits if the situation dictated retreat. I volunteered to enter the restaurant, as did Lt. Newsome, John, Bob R and Alan. We strategically placed ourselves around the restaurant as to have all vantage points covered. We all observed the major violator walk into McDonald's. He was supposed to be alone but he had four friends with him. One of his associates was a short, black male. He was wearing a red and white stripped shirt and baggy jeans. His 5'6", unthreatening frame contradicted the ferocious stare he wore. Another associate was 6'4" and of a muscular build. We grew steadily and almost unbearably uncomfortable with what appeared to be inevitable. The defendant did not have a kilogram of cocaine. This was a rip. The major violator and his associates placed themselves throughout the restaurant. He and the short one sat together. The big guy walked around the restaurant and finally stood in line as if he was going to order food. I stood and walked towards the bathroom. I passed the major violator and the short one and noticed a bulge on the right side of the short one's shirt near his pants. I went to the bathroom and immediately notified Fred that the "our guy" was at the McDonald's. The undercover agent was notorious for being late for jobs and, thankfully, he was late today.

When I returned to my seat, noticeable anxiety began consuming the bad guy and his associates. He could be overheard saying "He'll be here, just chill!" The short one did not wish to wait. He motioned to his crew and they all left McDonald's. Our "bad guy" remained. He waited patiently for the undercover. When the undercover agents finally arrived, the situation was less volatile. The agents sat with the "bad guy" at the table. The bad guy then went outside and made a call from his cellular phone. When he returned, he pled with the undercover agents to wait for the "package." Lt. Newsome called Fred and told Fred to call the operation. Fred placed a call to the undercover agent pager and they both left the restaurant. This job was over.

We arrested the bad guy two blocks from the McDonald's without major incident. During the interrogation he admitted to not having the cocaine. He also admitted that his intention was to rob our undercover. Had our undercover agent been on time, there would have been a shootout in McDonald's. After learning of the defendant's intentions, Fred wanted to discuss the day's enforcement operation.

"Anyone have anything to say about today?" he asked, hoping his invitation would be declined. We all looked at each other, the rank and file, using police officer telepathy to discuss what transpired. All our faces said, "It was a fucked up job", but our mouths remained silent. Finally, I spoke.

"Well, Fred, the job was poorly planned and executed.

You should have canceled the job because you knew that it sounded funny that this guy could come up with a kilo of coke. Especially after he burned us the first time."

My peripheral vision allowed me to notice that John nodded with assent to my remarks. I watched Fred while he acknowledged John's agreement.

"Fred, you should have just put the job on ice from the beginning", I continued. "We all could have gotten hurt really bad today. I know our undercover felt safe because I wasn't sitting too far from him. But inside surveillance didn't feel that good. We needed to know what was happening outside. Communication was really bad. We need to work on that."

Little else was said and Fred seemingly accepted my comments as constructive. One month later, I was transferred to Group Four. My third transfer/assignment within a year. Sweeney issued the transfer memorandum Friday afternoon before a three day holiday weekend. The day the memorandum was presented to me, Sweeney was on annual leave. I went to Fred who denied any culpability or knowledge that I was being transferred.

"Can I take my case."

"Sure, Maurice. You're the only one that knows it.", Fred responded.

I found it extraordinary that I was evaluated as an "outstanding" agent by supervisory personnel yet I was being moved with the frequency of a problem inmate. It was uniquely abnormal to move a special agent three times in a year. I had gone from investigating methamphetamine cases to the task force to background investigations and finally to another group. It fostered no consistency or camaraderie.

Laura Micheals was the supervisor of Group four. She was a severely thin woman whose head size reflected her extensive knowledge of DEA manuals and directives. During my initial meeting with Laura, she let me know that I had been pegged as a person with an "A" personality. Laura was a self proclaimed "smoozer" which meant she used diplomacy in place of talent. She reviewed the several cases I brought from Group six and spoke highly of the manner with which those cases were maintained. She was pleased that all paperwork associated with the case was present. Laura almost appeared surprised. She assigned me to "help" an older Philadelphia policeman, Ira, with his paper work and cases "because his paper is woefully deficient." She apparently did not have the time to help Ira or assign another agent to assist him. Ira was black and maybe that was enough. Whatever the reason, Ira and I formed a partnership. Ira was much older than I. He was near the mandatory age for retirement. I relied on Ira to provide information about Laura since he had been in her group for almost two years.

"She knows the paper but she don't know shit about the streets!" Ira spoke quickly and often shuddered like an old southern man. Because he did not know DEA's paperwork, he was perceived as useless and not a threat. Accordingly, people would have discussion in his presence as if he were not there. Ira had a wealth of information about people. In turn for helping him learn the paper, Ira helped me identify and deal with the dynamics in Group Four.

Before leaving group six, Fred gave me a copy of a Newark agent's early GS-13 promotional package. He said that the cases I had thus far would definitely qualify me for early promotion. After reading the agent's package, it so happened that the agent was white, I concurred with Fred. I made a copy of the package then adjusted my cases to fit the format used in the successful submission. After being assigned to Group Four, I presented my package to Laura who excitedly endorsed the submission and forwarded the package to Assistant Special

Agent in Charge (ASAC) Michael Treswick. Later that day, Laura advised me that Treswick believed that the package would not be approved by Sweeney.

"How does he know that, Laura?" I asked

"That's what he said. He said that there were not enough arrest." she replied.

I darted a look of confused anger in her direction which was a natural reflex in response to her remarks. The package was a mirrored image of the one that had been approved in Washington for the white agent from Newark. How can an ASAC not forward this package, I thought. It is for the SAC to determine the merit of a promotion package. My package not being properly adjudicated conjured feelings of calculated racial repression that my father spoke of. I felt betrayed, belittled and besieged. I contained my feelings of discontent until opportunity presented itself.

Fred was the acting ASAC, temporarily replacing Treswick while he was on leave. While Fred wobbled through the task force office, I called to him.

"Hey, Fred. How are you?" I tried my best to sound and appear genuine.

"Okay, Maurice. What's going on?" Fred took a nearby seat and rolled it to the side of my desk. He sat.

"I put my package together. I think it's pretty good."

"Let me take a look." As Fred reviewed the package, I continued to speak.

"Yeah. Treswick didn't let Sweeney see it. I don't know why because I thought it was pretty good myself."

"I agree, Maurice. You want me to take it up front? I see Laura has already endorsed it." He held the package like a baton, seeming eager to pass it forward to Sweeney.

"Yeah, if you don't mind."

"No problem, Maurice. No problem." Fred stood up in an

abrupt, agile motion that gave credibility to his claim of being a standout high school football player.

That day I learned that strange alliances are formed because of ambition. What I did not determine or even consider was Fred's reason for helping me. I had not pegged him as a philanthropist but an opportunist. Fred carried and maintained ulterior motives like they were a collection of antique vehicles. My sense of logical deduction had been veiled by what I knew I deserved: promotion to GS-13. Yet, I had not even been presented with clear and legitimate explanation as to why I could not be promoted. I would not accept the ASAC's 'Barry won't sign off on it' rejoinder to my package. I wanted to know what the SAC had to say. I wanted him to review the package and make a determination. Now it would be done.

Two days later, I received an answer. Laura stormed past the group into her office after meeting with Sweeney. She emphatically slammed the door. I noticed the flushness of her face. It was as if someone painted her red. I knew it was me. She said not a word but I knew. I had not seen Fred since I gave him the package. That was a disturbing indicator as to what happened. Laura's tirade further justified my assumption. She remained in her office for hours. I remained at my desk. Finally, when everyone else left, her door opened. After noticing we were alone, she spoke freely.

"Why did you do that?" she said, obviously consumed with anger.

"Do what?" I replied in an arrogant fashion.

"You had Fred take that package up front after me and Treswick told you that Sweeney would not sign it!" Her professional demeanor had diminished considerably.

"Well, why wouldn't he sign it?" I barked.

"Treswick told me that you didn't have enough arrests!" she said reciprocating my vocal performance.

"And what the fuck did Sweeney say. Did he say anything? Hell, Laura, you got yours. It's not a big deal for you. It is for me because I know I should have it. I should be promoted and I don't need a drunk to tell me that the SAC won't sign off on it because he has that feeling. That's bullshit!" Laura's face became distorted with the combination of confusion and fury.

"You know what, Maurice. I want you out of my group."

"Gladly. I'll leave. I don't want to be here anyway." Upon that statement, Laura declined further eye contact. She appeared to be lost in contemplation like an expert chess player. I waited for her to raise her eyes but she did not. I left feeling alone, feeling denied, feeling conspired against. I needed help. The relationship between Laura and I became increasingly bitter and suspicious. Our augmenting animosity towards each other did not reflect in my evaluations. My work performance continued to be superior. However, I felt the pinch of negative perception via the grunts that would commit murder to get ahead. My attitude became worse. Intuition armed me with the sense of pending peril and ubiquitous distrust of co workers. I was being forced to make a move. I called Lewis Roberts.

Roberts had recently become the SAC of the New York Division. I wanted to personally congratulate him and wish him well in his new post. I also wanted words of encouragement and wisdom. In the past, Roberts had always been receptive to my complaints and concerns regarding the agency.

"Hey there, Mr. Roberts. What's happening?"

"Young Maurice Williamson. How are you?" Roberts always used "young" as a qualifier for my name. I never liked it but accepted it as a term of endearment, not a criticism or indication of my experience.

"Hanging tough, you know. Congrats on becoming SAC. I was hoping you would come back here. I need that friend up front."

"Yeah, it's nice to be home." Roberts was originally from New York. "Everything going well?" he asked.

"It's alright", I lied. "I'll be in New York tomorrow. I have to drop some drugs off at the lab. Will you be around?"

"For you, young Maurice Williamson, I'll make some time." Roberts was being good natured when he qualified my name, but the feeling of subordination that resulted augmented my sense of impending martyrdom.

"See you tomorrow then, sir."

When I arrived in New York, I went directly to Roberts's office. We made conversation pertaining to the drug exhibit I had in my possession. Then Roberts boasted in a juvenile manner that I had never seen.

"Yeah, young Maurice Williamson. How you like this office." The office was nice but I had never been enthralled with position or personal property. My return look reflected that opinion. I was more impressed with what I believed Roberts was. That is, a person with conviction and dedication. As he showed me the personal bathroom (I guess SACs can't shit with us mere mortals), Roberts was able to recognize that I was unmoved.

"Well, it's not much, especially compared to Barry's office."

That comment replaced my boredom with inquisitiveness.

"You know Barry Sweeney?" I asked already knowing the answer. I was hoping that would prompt Roberts to speak further about Sweeney.

"Oh, yeah. We go way back. He used to be my supervisor when I first started in New York." Roberts was a very young SAC. He was about 43 and appeared to be younger. Sweeney was about 55 and was rumored to be the next SAC of New York. Instead, he remained in Philadelphia and Roberts was anointed the "super" SAC of New York. New York is the largest division in DEA and the most visible. Everyone in DEA knows who the SAC of New York is, just like they know who the Administrator is. Sweeney, who happened to be very friendly with Thomas Constatine, DEA's Administrator, who was also a former New York State Trooper, must have believed that the New York SAC position was a certainty. That disappointment was a realization that he had gone as far as he was going in DEA. For Roberts, a former subordinate, to be selected to such a powerful position, one that dwarfed Sweeney's, was an arduous task for someone from Sweeney's era and ethnicity.

"I spoke to Barry not too long ago regarding a job one of my agents has that stretches to Philly", Roberts continued. "I asked him how you were doing."

Oh, shit, I thought.

"What did he say," I asked.

"He said you had a good case and that you were working it well", Roberts nonchalantly stated. "You ever think about coming to New York? It's a lot of work up here."

"I thought about it, but the commute is a mother."

"That's right. You live in South Jersey. I know a few people that make that commute, though."

I had a second child on the way and had listened intently to how this job had ruined marriages and relationships. I did not want to be an absentee father too tired to make it home to hold my daughter or kiss my wife. Two hundred miles a day was a little more than I was willing to travel, even for the security that Roberts could provide. I wanted my family near me and my wife wanted to work.

"What do you think about Sweeney, Mr. Roberts?" I said changing the subject. Mr. Roberts looked at me as if to say, "Didn't I just tell you?" He raised his eyebrows and began to recite Sweeney's resume. He told me where Sweeney worked, when Sweeney worked there and his general perception of Sweeney.

M

"Sweeney is a political animal. He expects loyalty. He also has problems with minorities."

"I'm having a slight problem with him now." I submitted.

"Promotion, right?"

"Yeah, that's right."

"How long have you been on the job, six years?"

I nodded affirmatively.

"Well, Sweeney is notorious for holding back the promotions of black agents. Tell you what, Maurice, think some more about New York. I'll be down there soon and we can talk about it.

"You have time for lunch?" Roberts asked.

I did not have any money on me so a free lunch was welcomed. After lunch I returned to the Philly Office where I meditated at my desk. I pondered everything that Roberts said and everything he did not say. A move was necessary. Roberts knew I should have been promoted to the GS-13 level at this point in my career. I watched as white agents received their promotions early, before the normal five year period, by submitting paperwork supporting their achievements. I tried the same thing with better cases and hit an unmovable wall. He was trying to pull me under his wing, again. This time, I would be prepared for those who say I am a "brown noser" or I am kissing butt to get ahead. It would definitely be the path of least resistance to travel to New York for the support Roberts could give me. But I have a family now. I have to prioritize.

CHAPTER V

/.V.\

DEA HAS AN ENTITY called the Equal Employment Opportunity Monitoring Committee. That committee consists of senior level black DEA employees who convey discrimination concerns from minority employees to the agency via attorneys. To my knowledge, they attempt to reach solutions to discrimination claims informally with DEA. A member of that committee, Wanda Fredricks, heard my complaints and agreed to have the committee hear them. I had Wanda's ear because we were once an item and somehow remained friends. I did not know the members of the committee nor did I try to learn about them. My purpose was pursued with a single mindedness that rivaled that of a starved predator. What I did not know was that the committee was full of black Fred Palumbo's. Everyone had their own agenda and if discussing people's problems or claims, which by rules of EEO disclosure should be kept in confidence, would gain them favor, they would do so with uncaring, intentional fluidity.

When my complaints were raised at the committee meeting, all members, especially Rose Clayton, ASAC in Los Angeles, agreed they were legitimate. Rose Clayton called to advise me that the committee was going to further investigate my accusations. That call prompted me to conduct research on Rose Clayton. Rose had an extensive, combative history with DEA. She had once been fired but battled to get her job back. She overtly expressed her opinions in a manner that beckoned responses from the agency. She was well respected and her trials with DEA made her a matriarch to younger agents and a beacon for stubborn dogma. I welcomed the inquiry and offered to provide her and the committee with any information they needed.

One person that vouched for the effective and sincerity of Rose Clayton was Bob Rogers. I had worked with Bob as he was a member of Lt. Newsome's group. He was the DEA supervisor of Group 5. The entire task force recognized Bob as a knowledgeable agent and someone they would not be hesitant to hit a door with. Bob was also a lawyer. His status as such precluded him from many of the petty games that management played with others. The EEO committee was actively recruiting Bob to become a member of the group. Bob was unsure because he believed that the committee was "a lot of talk without results." However, after observing the disparage and openly contentious treatment I received from divisional management, Bob felt that he could convincingly and forcefully relay the atmosphere in which he and I was working. Bob and I would talk for hours at a time about the how the agency operated regarding black, white promotions. He could further make it clear to the committee that there was absolutely no reason for me to be denied promotion. Thus, Bob joined the committee and made presentations on my behalf. The committee met once a quarter in Washington. Bob's first meeting was in October. He called me from D.C. to keep me abreast of the process.

"Hey, Maurice. What's going on?" Bob spoke in a voice that was proper and conjured images of a white male.

"Nothing much. Just doing the paper from the key that snitch bought the other day." I responded.

"Oh, yeah. That was a great job but I told you that already. What are you going to do next?"

"I'll probably try to identify a few more guys in Virginia then take it down. I don't want to do a wire. Too damn time consuming."

"Sounds good. I met with Rose today." I leaned back in my chair waiting to hear what happened. "Actually, I met with the entire committee. Rose was very vocal about her feelings for Sweeney."

"What do you mean?" I asked.

"She does not like Barry Sweeney. Apparently, they have a history. The first thing she said to me when I came through the door was 'What the hell is going on in Philly? That damn Barry Sweeney is up to his old game again. He's always been a racist and I guess he just can't stop. Is he that bad?' That caught me off guard because I don't know who's in the room. You know what I mean?"

"I hear you", I said feeling confident that I was not alone in my assessment of Sweeney.

"Here's the bottom line. They want you to put together a chronology of employment with DEA. Make sure to include the transfers. We're going to make a presentation to Chief Counsel Cindy Rosen and to the Director of Operation George Williamson. Get that to me by 10:00 a.m. tomorrow."

"You'll have it, Bob. Is that it?"

"Well, let's just say you have a captive audience. Make it good."

I drafted what was requested and sent it to Bob at 9 the next morning. Bob called me again at 3 that afternoon.

"They all believe that Sweeney has a personal problem with you." Bob reported.

"Who is they? George and Cindy Rosen?"

"Yes. Based on your evaluations and your record as an agent, there was no reason to deny your promotion." Bob seemed very excited to report those findings.

"Bet! What's next then?" I curiously asked.

"George Williamson is going to discuss this issue with Sweeney and get back to Rose. We'll take it from there."

"That's good news, Bob. I'll talk to you when you get back."

When I hung up the phone, I felt a degree of accomplishment that warranted an early exit home. I had taken a position and remained steadfast in obtaining my goal: promotion. I did not consider the repercussions that were a certainty when accusing and proving that a high ranking official did not temper his promotional decisions with equity and impartiality. I simply knew that Sweeney had no reasonable rational for denying my promotion. My white peers were promoted without commotion or ordeal. That right, to be easily promoted perpetuated disparate treatment between blacks and whites. People in the agency that make policy were the ones who were promoted. I wanted to be a shot caller. I made no secret of my intentions. I was willing to challenge the agency with a slingshot and one rock.

I called my father periodically to advise him on how things were going. He would listen intently to my verbal tirades as I tried to make him feel the sting of covert discrimination. I did not have to complain much. He was very familiar with discrimination, both covert and overt. So, after one of many remonstrative rants that focused on the agency and their promotion policy my father interjected his opinion, laced with wisdom that was not received.

"Yeah, Pop. I'm telling you. They don't want blacks up there because they know we will change things. You know, make them fair."

"And what's wrong with that?" he responded with a hint of disbelief.

"What do you mean what's wrong with that, Pop? Everything is wrong with that. If a person is worthy of something, they should get it. They should not be allowed to, without punishment, put who they want in positions they want them in. That's not right, Pop."

"Uh-huh", he interjected.

"You don't think I was right, calling them on the carpet regarding my promotion?"

"The question is whether or not it was smart, not right."

"Alright, Pop, what should I have done then? Should I have just taken it, accepted it and moved on? Or should I have made them recognize by letting them know that I should be a 13?" There was a long, uncomfortable pause on the telephone. It was the type of pause that invoked memories of phone conversations that my father and I had following school suspensions or other juvenile indiscretions. I would, in vain, attempt to justify my position knowing full well that my father was going to beat me when he arrived home. Strangely, I got that identical heart pounding, butt warming feeling that I did as youth while listening to the silence on the phone. During the silence, I recalled the feeling of imminent fear and trepidation that my father's presence caused when I was younger. I remember wanting to please him but, being unable to, disliking him. Our relationship only recently evolved to sincere exchange of thoughts and life experience. I had been conditioned to believe that I was "stupid" or "dumb" by his repetitive and successful attempts to deny self confidence. It was only recently, after my three year old disbursed urine throughout the house, that I understood that words from stressed out, discriminated against black men with a family to support and an omnipresent feeling of underachievement, are expressions of what those men do not want their children to be. It is a temporary lapse in judgment and hope that understanding life's challenges will be transferred to ignorant youth. My father eased his onslaughts of abusive words after I went to college. I did not see him that often and that was the primary reason. But when I became an agent and had a child, our relationship became friendly. I realized that his obdurate behavior was a role that parents play to maintain appropriate separation between parent and child. For the child however, it is difficult to disclose thoughts when parent-child relationship was based on parental deference and child subordination. Finally, I was at that junction where I understood my father and his motives. It was amazing how quickly I regressed from that light of knowledge during our silence to the youthful lament of impending criticism. My father spoke.

"If you were in power, wouldn't you want people around you that thought like you? How else would you plan to make progress? For example, you said numerous times that if you were the boss, you would make sure that you hired many blacks. You would still do that?"

"Yes."

"Then tell me again what's wrong with what he's doing? He don't want to promote you because you made it clear that you and he don't think alike."

"But if he would have just given me my due, I wouldn't have to drop dimes to headquarters. I just want to be promoted."

"You better just make sure your ass is clean, boy. People like that will retaliate. And listen, I'm not saying you're wrong, because you're not. Just remember what I said and now, watch yourself because it's not over. It's his turn."

His comments accelerated the brevity of my glory. I now felt that I had done something wrong.

M

"So when you going to the doctor, Pop?" I countered wanting to make him as uncomfortable as I.

My mother told me that my father was always tired. He complained to my mother but did not let anyone else know. My mother felt something was wrong and that he needed to see a doctor.

"Oh, I don't know. Whenever I'm able to get out the bed", he responded in a fatigued voice.

"If you don't go, how you gonna know what's wrong with you. It's not natural to be tired all the time."

"I know. I know. I'll get there next week", he said as if trying to change the subject.

My father had a history of high blood pressure. In fact, he once survived a heart attack. Was that the cost of subscribing to his doctrine of how to deal with powerful people and bureaucracies? He drank, he smoked and he partied. Migraines would grip him so tightly that when younger I observed my father, after work, ascend the stairs and enter his bedroom closing the door behind him and remaining in a dark room until we had all eaten so he could be alone. No one dared enter the room or make loud cries of youthful enthusiasm. My siblings and I had been conditioned to remain silent when Pop entered the house without speaking. Beatings will do that.

"I think you should go to the doctor like now. If you need me to take you, let me know." My father did not respond to my statement.

"I have to arrest some people tomorrow morning so my day will be over early. I'll come by and maybe we'll get some breakfast. How's that sound?"

"No, not tomorrow. I got some things to do."

"What you got to do, Pop?"

"I might go to the Y."

M

I realized that he did not want to see me, so I hung up the phone without saying good-bye. I sat motionless decoding what Pop said. I was able to surmise his prophetic vision: I was in trouble. I was unaware however, that attacking a SAC creates plenty of enemies, not just an individual. Thus I did not know where to find the source of my father's revelation.

When I returned to work the following day, I had a memorandum on my desk, signed by Sweeney, transferring me to another group: Group III. There were no reasons stated. It was the SAC's discretion. For the fourth time in a year and a half, I had been transferred. Laura was very apologetic though I realized that as soon as I left her office, she would laugh hysterically at my misfortune. Group III was a Mobile Enforcement Group (MET). That meant that I would travel to small municipalities to assist with their large drug problem. While the purpose appears noble, I knew that my role was limited. I was to be the undercover operative. I was to sacrifice my life for nickel and dime bags. Furthering investigations was not a priority. The MET group simply spent money and assisted the police department. In most cases, the smaller departments and their narcotics squad were manned by white officers. Most of these officers did not understand, nor had they ever acted, in an undercover capacity. They naturally assumed that I, a black federal narcotics agent, had an expertise in purchasing drugs. I was to be utilized primarily for that purpose. They believed that because of my skin color, I could gain access to areas other agents (white) could not. The irony of DEA was that many of the agents came from small police departments where racial stereotypes are the norm. They never voiced their opinions, but it was divulged through body language and what was not said.

I met with the supervisor of the MET group that same day. His name was Steve. Steve was a tall man with a deep voice and hard Boston accent. Every time I saw him, I saw a redneck personified. He looked and sounded the part. When he spoke I winced. I knew that he became a supervisor via the old boy network and extensive charity from SAC Sweeney. Sweeney anointed him the Supervisor of the Technical Operation group even though he had no experience in the area. After he was made acting supervisor, Steve went to Washington for the supervisor's assessment. Potential supervisors are given scenarios that they must complete that are related to the duties and the situations they may encounter as a GS-14. Steve's score was not impressive but he was given the Group III supervisor's position by Sweeney. This was in spite of having individuals in the Philadelphia office with higher assessment scores and proven leadership abilities. One of those people was Bob Rogers, the man that through his actions pledged to help me become a GS-13.

I was not completely opposed to conducting undercover negotiations. However, I did not want that to be the sole purpose for my existence. The only way I would be able to determine what Steve wanted from me was to watch his reaction to my declination of undercover work. During our conversation, I let him know.

"Maurice. Welcome to the group", he said as he greeted me with a handshake in his office. "I know it was a surprise to you to get transferred here but we have some good things going. We're in Norristown now and we have a pretty good snitch."

"So what have you done so far?" I inquired already knowing the answer.

"We have a wealth of information that we need to investigate", Steve replied after sipping his coffee.

"Well, I just want you to know that I am not interested right now in doing undercover. I was just on a huge case and I need to regain my focus."

Steve wanted to take a sip of his coffee but my words appeared to cause a halt to his basic mechanical skills. He frowned and placed his cup on his desk. For twenty seconds, he chocked on his attempts to speak.

"We need to go see Sanchez about this."

I was right. I had been pegged to buy narcotics, not to be a case agent; a title and degree of responsibility to which I had grown accustomed.

"Let's go", I said returning his request with a wide-eyed look that could be easily mistaken for arrogance.

As we walked to the front office, I felt a peculiar emotion rage my thoughts. It was feeling suspended between the pride of a martyr and the reality of my $72,000 a year job; the romantic feeling that follows an act of courage versus the reality of being further blackballed. I was still not flexible enough to balance the two. It would be one or the other. My position would not fluctuate. My resolve not to perform undercover was increasingly piloted by an uncompromising attitude guided by the world of right and wrong. I had determined that it was time for white agents to step up and risk their lives in an undercover capacity. Every step towards the front office allowed me time to determine how to couch such a notion. Sanchez, although Hispanic, was frequently referred to as "Uncle Pedro, a Hispanic version of "Uncle Tom." That eliminated a direct approach. Saying what they already knew to be true would not help me in this situation. When we arrived at Sanchez's office, Sanchez actually seemed pleased to see me.

"Hey, Maurice. Welcome to your new group", Sanchez said.

"Thank you, sir. Happy to be here", I replied.

"Well, sir", Steve interjected and his voice alone was enough to ruin the friendly atmosphere Sanchez and I attempted to manufacture. "Maurice seems to be very apprehensive about undercover work."

"Well, I wouldn't say apprehensive. I've done enough not to be caught up with fear. I would say that I am just drained right now and need time to get my bearings. I had a big case going and, well, I'm just a little tired and frustrated that I won't be able to dedicate significant time to it."

"I see", Sanchez said. "Why don't we do this. Take some time and get familiar with the group and what their doing. Then, you can do undercover. That's all you would have to do. After you write the reports, you can come back to the office and work on the other case. How's that sound?"

It sounded just right. I would be able to work my "baby" and all I had to do was buy some dope. I could not let them know I was excited so I hid that emotion behind an intense empty stare.

"Let me get comfortable with the group and we'll go from there", I said.

Everyone agreed. I left the office and was internally engaged with satisfaction. I returned to my desk with a smile. Then, suddenly, satisfaction left with the speed of a fleeting mid-day summer storm. It was replaced by the blinding light of contemplation that reminded me of the last time I was compromised by the front office. Satisfaction vacated my mind and was quickly supplanted with the vulnerable sensation that Sweeney had once given me. If I performed undercover, I believed that I would, again, be selling out. Even the prospect of finishing the case I started could not squelch the feeling that being untrue to one's self creates.

I called Bob, who was still in Washington to ask him what was going on.

"I heard, Maurice. The MET group, huh?" he joked.

"That shit ain't funny, man. I don't feel like traveling around to all these redneck counties where all they want to do is lock up a brother. What happened down there?" I said waiting for a reply.

"The long and short of it is this." Bob paused as if proper wording was essential. "George Williamson called Sweeney and asked him about your situation. Apparently, Sweeney told him you were a problem. When George asked him why you weren't promoted, he also let Sweeney know that he had your package in front of him, Sweeney said you did not have the 'breadth of experience'."

I consumed this report like I was taking a long drag on a cigarette.

"What is breadth of experience?" I asked knowing Bob had no answer.

"No one knows. We've been trying to figure that out. Cindy Rosen (Chief Counsel) was also confused as to why you weren't promoted. She said, and I quote, 'There is definitely a personal problem between Sweeney and this agent. 'This agent' being you. The one conclusion we have come to is that Sweeney doesn't like you very much."

When Bob concluded, the phone remained stuck to my ear in disbelief. Then Bob spoke again.

"He has two weeks to respond in writing to George Williamson about your promotion. We have to wait until then."

Two weeks to explain breadth of experience and why I did not have it after being in four different groups in less than two years. More urgent, however, was the avoidance of undercover work. I fished for every reason possible to avoid undercover work. Ironically, senior group members insisted that during surveillance, I be the one closest to the snitch because I could "fit in." What was absent from their logic was that any person or vehicle that was not escorted by an individual from a neighborhood would be deemed as an outsider. Color was insignificant. A black male with his baseball cap turned backward would be just as much of a foreigner as a white man in a suit and in many cases, even more so. It was also paradoxical that senior criminal investigators would want to place their future undercover operative so close to a confidential informant while that informant was gathering information from potential defendants; defendants I was supposed to eventually meet. Despite my insincere efforts to dissuade these investigators that being tasked as the primary eyeball for the group could limit my undercover effectiveness, they remained firm in their asinine position. I hoped that the entire neighborhood would recognize my government vehicle as being incongruous with its surroundings. That would burn me and eliminate any chance I had to perform undercover without being insubordinate.

Case agents for the Norristown operation divvied out assignments before each operation. The confidential informant was trying to purchase an ounce of cocaine. Again, they wanted me to be the primary eye. That day, however, I was wearing a sweatshirt that had a law enforcement emblem on it. When I brought the shirt to their attention, they seemed unmoved by its presence and the potential problems it could cause. Instead, they temporarily assigned me another vehicle that had even darker tinted windows than the government vehicle I had. When I entered the car, I could hardly see out of the window. The fact that it was dusk also contributed to the lack of visibility. I turned my sweatshirt inside out and proceeded to park my vehicle in an area where I could see the snitch but was inconspicuous. I was noticed almost immediately.

"This is 305", I said using the portable radio and using my call number so that the surveillance team knew who was speaking. "This is a bad location. People are looking at the car." There was about a twenty second pause, then 302 spoke.

"Stay there right now because the snitch is on his way in. Nobody else has an eye on the area. 10-4", said 302.

"10-4", I said with a hint of resignation.

ΛΛ

As the snitch walked into the area, I saw him speak to a group of three or four black males that pointed in my direction. The snitch then began to stroll toward the block where I was. He was stopped at the corner of the block by a short, thin black male that also pointed in my direction. I was made.

"302, I think you need to get someone else to take the eye. Is anybody in position yet?" My tone advised 302 that there was a problem.

"305, can you stay a little longer? He's meeting with the main target."

I placed my gun on my lap. When I was about to respond to 302, five kids, maybe eleven years of age, began knocking on the car's window. I knew they could not see inside the window because of the tint. However, my lack of an assertive response to the repeated knocks on the window let them know exactly who I was. I pulled away to the children chiming "Five-O. Five-O." The snitch even joined in not wanting his actual intentions disclosed.

"I had to leave the area 302. They started knocking on the window. 10-4."

"Yeah. Return back to the meet spot. 10-4."

"10-4."

The operation ended shortly after I left the area and my wait at the meet location was short. When the entire group returned, the snitch told them that they had seen my shirt and knew I was a cop. When I heard him, I quickly challenged him.

"Motherfucker, can't nobody see through that damn window. Even if they looked hard, they couldn't see."

"I'm telling you, man, they saw your shirt."

I began to torture myself for bringing the shirt to the group's attention in front of the snitch. I gave them a free-bee. Still, it was turned inside out and it could not have been noticed. Fortunately, I did not hear a word about it. The shirt was a non-factor. During mid-year evaluations, Steve, despite my inactivity in regard to undercover work, stated that I was "a very professional agent" and that he "could not recommend any changes in my work or attitude."

/\/\

CHAPTER VI

⋀

THREE WEEKS PASSED AND THERE WAS NO NEWS from George Williamson. I was becoming more and more discouraged and resigned that there would be no promotion for me. Moreover, I was now a lamb walking through a den of starved lions without the cover of a flock to distract attention from me. I needed to make a positive impact. I had been stripped of my career case and was at the mercy of the group supervisor to make me a case agent. Becoming a case agent in the MET group was an assignment given by the group supervisor. No undercover, no case agent. Then I received a call from Mike, the snitch from my big case. It was as unexpected as the first time that he called but welcomed for nostalgic sake. We exchanged greetings and I described for him the type of group to which I belonged. Mike told me of the headaches he was having with Laura in an attempt to finish the case I started.

"Sure wish I could work with you, Maurice, because I met a few guys that move a lot of weight", Mike despondently stated.

"What do they move?" I asked anxiously.

"More coke than heroin, but a lot of both", Mike confidently said.

"Can they bring it to Wilmington?"

⋀

"Sure they can. They run a pipeline that stretches from Florida to New York. Why? I thought you couldn't do anything."

"Well, Mike, I can if they can do it in Wilmington. That's where we'll be next. Let me talk to my supervisor and I'll call you back."

When I hung up the phone, I sprang from my desk and bounced to Steve's office like a fresh boxer. I knew he would resist any ideal that would shine a positive light upon me. Not only did I not perform undercover, but I brought attention to the man that made him a supervisor. Still, I would try to explore Steve's more reasonable faculties despite his IQ being identical to that of a 2 X 4.

"Hey, Steve. I think I may have something."

"What do you have, Maurice?" Every motion Steve made, from placing down his pen to sitting back in his chair, revealed his reluctance to entertain my ideals.

"I just got a call from the snitch that I used in that case I had from Group four. He told me that he knew some guys that could supply large amounts of heroin and cocaine. They're Italian, possibly mob guys. Any way, he said he could set something up."

"We can't do any long term investigations. Besides, we are going to Wilmington next. If it doesn't happen in Wilmington, we can't do it."

"I know that, Steve. He said he could make it happen in Wilmington. I'll just do a work up on the guys he mentioned and see what else I can find out. The snitch is in Florida now so he knows the guys. It shouldn't be that hard."

"We're really strapped for manpower now. I don't think we'll have the resources to do that job."

"I'll give it to someone who has the time and resources. Is that alright with you?" I sarcastically uttered.

"That's fine, Maurice", Steve voiced with a great degree of finality.

I went to Lt. Newsome with the information and explained to him what I explained to Steve. He was excited about the information. I told him that the informant was in Florida and I could make arrangements for a meeting at the office. Lt. Newsome agreed. He knew of the informant's track record from the case I had. Lt. Newsome's only concern was that Mike did not expect payment for his travel; unless, of course, the information Mike provided was useful. I agreed. I called Mike from Lt. Newsome's office and explained to Mike what the expectations were. I told him he would only receive money for his travel if his information was "good." Mike agreed and a date for the meeting was scheduled.

My father's condition was worsening. Before my eyes, he was slowly falling victim to an unnamed slayer. He had become languid and had the strength or rather inclination to do nothing more than switch channels with the remote control. On occasion, when he did muster the vitality to exit the house, he would go to "church" and drink alcohol until his sobriety matched his verve. His mind, however, was still sharp. He had ample opinion for my situation. When I told him I had been transferred, he was not surprised.

"Well, what did you expect, boy? They are going to come after you with guns blazin'. You called them on the carpet. Now they have to make you suffer", My father said with the certainty of a preacher giving the Sunday sermon.

"Well, Pop, I had to do what I had to do. They were supposed to get back to me regarding my promotion four weeks ago. I haven't heard a thing."

"You won't hear a thing until they want you to hear something."

"Pop. They had no cause to do this to me."

"To do what? Shit, boy! You work for them!"

"No, Pop. I work for the government and I know full well how I should be performing. And I was doing just that."

Then, suddenly, the dichotomy of my father's words rendered me speechless. I became confused. This man had taught me that things are either right or wrong. There was no in between. Now I was constantly being bombarded with gray, while seeking the comfort my father taught me was intertwined with being right. I was alarmed at my father's political awareness and why he had not bestowed such talents on me. My father was fanatical with rules and obsessed with punishment. There never appeared the light of compassion or compromise. From my juvenile eyes, life was a series of black and white events. I got in trouble at school, I got beat. There were no questions when it came to rendering the consequences of my actions. My father was precise and mechanical about that duty. The only conversation we had regarding discipline was a succinct explanation as to why the beating was necessary. This conversation was often more painful than the beating itself; anticipation has a way heightening the experience. My father's history, and sadly his pedigree, and his current ideology forced my perception of him to be an oxymoron personified. I could not call him a hypocrite despite feeling that way. Respect would not allow it and I was unsure how such comments would be met. But I had to let him know that what he taught me and what he was saying were two different ideologies. Today was not the day, however, so I remained suspended between two schools of thoughts: one that was beaten into me and one that was new.

There was an undercurrent of deception in the office after Mike met with Lt. Newsome. Laura saw Mike and was aggressive in her inquisition as to his presence in the Philadelphia office. Lt. Newsome called to advise me that Laura was pissed.

"Maurice, Laura is very upset. She damn near turned into a beet when she saw the CI."

I was not quite sure why Laura would be upset. An informant is the property of DEA, not a particular group.

"So what. She has no idea how to run a case, that's why he called me with info instead of calling her", I responded.

"Well, just so you know, she asked a lot of questions and wanted to know why he was here. I told her that he had information that was relevant to one of our investigations. She was peeved, but she let it go."

"Was it good information he gave you?" I said.

"It was useful."

That was the bottom line. I was able to supply viable narcotics information to a group within DEA that had the time to pursue it. My group was unable to because of supervisory induced restrictions. The slight of my former group and Laura, while unintentional, was a fringe benefit of Lt. Newsome's group starting a new case. Because the Lt. was black and because Bob was in that group, I extended my loyalties to them. I was hoping that Mike could give them information that would balloon into the type of investigation I had when I utilized his services. I did not consider that Lt. Newsome was "on loan" from the Philadelphia Police Department and any unfavorable comments to the commissioner from Sweeney would speed his departure from the Task Force. Bob was directly under Sweeney's control. Shortly after this incident, he reminded Bob who was in charge.

Bob was transferred, unexpectedly, to my group. The MET group. Again, the memorandum was issued on the Thursday before a three day weekend. Apropos, Sweeney was on annual leave that Friday thus avoiding the first wave of emotional contact. Bob was marinating in discord, however. He had served as acting supervisor for more than a year before

Lt. Newsome arrived, yet never received GS-14 pay; a slight that seemed reserved for black agents but conspicuously absent for white agents. That is, whenever a white agent was an acting supervisor, he received supervisory pay without question. Sweeney apparently took pride in that. Tuesday could not arrive quickly enough for Bob. He carefully rehearsed his comments and we exchanged extensive dialogue about how DEA fostered and nurtured racism. When Tuesday came, Bob was in the front office before Sweeney. Sweeney did lend his ear to Bob's complaints and answered them without emotion: "Your transfer was for the betterment of the division." So Bob's resolve met the arrogance of complete control and both logic and reason were useless weapons against its domineering veil. So Bob became an even stronger crusader for right. The monitoring committee was meeting in a month. He and I meticulously chronicled the misfortunes of black agents in the Philadelphia field division. Unfortunately, other blacks that had problems remained silent seemingly comforted by the cushion of their plush salary. Bob's transfer was the SAC's discretion. That left me and my problems desolate. But I had already committed to voicing my concerns and could not renege.

When Bob left to go to Washington, I steered clear of contact with Steve. Annual evaluations were near and I did not want to further instigate an already unstable situation. I began to realize that my complaints were being used by the monitoring committee as a beacon of blatant discrimination that hamstrings competent blacks in DEA. Bob told me that the committee was meeting with the Administrator of DEA to discuss the issues surrounding my situation. I was becoming a sacrificial lamb.

Bob called me after the meeting with the Administrator. His voice was full of frustration and despair.

"You know what, Maurice. These guys are full of shit?" Bob whispered discernibly.

"What happened?" I sulked, knowing the meeting did not provide the expected results.

"He said that sometimes, supervisory officials are just being nice when they give evaluation, instead of truthful. In your situation, they were just being nice."

"What the hell does that mean?" I exclaimed. "I have been an outstanding agent for seven years. Is he saying that all the supervisors lied? They are full of shit. Now what, Bob?"

"I don't know. Sweeney never even called George William back. He went right to Administrator. He didn't call George because George's black. George told Rose (Rose Clayton, head of the EEO Monitoring Committee) that he could not touch the situation right now."

I heard Bob's voice rambling about the DEA and the old boy network, but I was listening to what my father told me about power. I played it over in my mind. I blamed him for not giving me the savvy to delicately manipulate situations. Right and wrong, right and wrong. That is all I knew. I was not prepared for this.

The onslaught began with a resounding blow from the Agency. Ten days after Bob returned from his meeting with the Administrator, I was given what was described as a "Warning" evaluation. It was saturated with deficiencies that predated my mid-year evaluation and was at best a harsh, abusive interpretation motivated by something other than the truth. The document was a flurry of slanted commentary aimed at demeaning the subject of the abuse. It worked. My less than zealous approach to performing undercover work, a task that is not mandated by DEA and rarely if ever performed by my white counterparts, was outlined in painstaking clarity. I was "disruptive" to enforcement actions because of declining undercover work. I was not "supportive" of the groups endeavor and purpose because I did not perform undercover. The sweatshirt issue in Norristown was also mentioned. Steve also documented Mike's trip to Philadelphia to meet with Lt. Newsome and how supervisory authorization had not been given. After reading the epic, some 25 pages of derogatory information, my esteem sank like a brick in a lake. I read the document in front of Sanchez and Steve. I attempted to mask my emotions but realized it was futile. All I hoped for was not to strike anyone or completely lose it.

"I know you don't want me to sign this." I indignantly stated.

"Maurice, it's up to you if you sign it or not. This is just to make you aware of where you are and the areas in which you will have to improve", Sanchez said. My stare was attached to his eyes. Every word he spoke augmented my already heightened degree of anger. He wore the smirk of satisfaction when he spoke obviously knowing that I had limited recourse. "And Maurice, did you read that second document?"

"What are you talking about?" Anger began to seep into my voice like water into a sponge.

"The second document assigns you to Bob Rogers for remedial training and closer supervision", Sanchez remarked calmly.

"Oh yeah", I said realizing that if I said anything it would be perceived exactly how I would want it to be. Steve sat in a supercilious fashion not saying a word the entire time. Steve knew they had his back. All he had to do was follow orders. After I read the "remedial" memorandum, I got up from the chair and walked toward the door.

"Before you leave, Maurice, we would like you to sign this document. It doesn't mean you agree with it but...."

That was all I heard from him because I continued to walk

without breaking stride or acknowledging Sanchez's request. I was so far beyond anger that I was calm. I began to accept my current situation as being warranted. I hit someone and they hit me back. Now I had to accept what was happening. I had the opportunity to remain silent but I did what I thought was right and necessary. I jousted all night with myself. I was tormented by conflicting ideals and pondered the outcome of each. I went to the strip club. A lap dance or two, a beer and anonymity usually cleared my head. Ronnie was there tonight. His familiar smile and embrace made me feel at home. He bought me a beer and we talked about nothing in particular. As I listened to him talk and observed my surroundings, I felt an almost magnetic draw to these surroundings: The smell of smoke and sweat, the wide-eyed look of first timers, the fine women. All of those elements provided me with a strong sense of belonging. The fact that Ronnie trusted me with his life was a plus. He told me that he recently "acquired" this bar and was looking for someone to evaluate the "talent." Ronnie knew how much I loved women. But I declined his offer, with a smile.

"Guess I have to do it all by myself!" he gleefully remarked. Ronnie knew something was wrong but he did not inquire. After my third beer, I left, promising to be there next week. I departed the bar and traveled home with the same thoughts I had when I left work. The recurring solution during the drive home was an emphatic "Fuck them motherfuckers." I had not devised a plan to make that thought one worth trying. Thus, I had to continue through this situation that was quickly becoming unbearable. My performance had never been questioned. Now, because I openly complained of the discriminatory promotion practices in DEA, I was marked for extermination.

While at the academy, instructors taught that during a

potentially dangerous situation, the best course of action is to eliminate the threat. That is what DEA brass was doing. Instead of dealing with a legitimate issue, they wanted to destroy the threat. Trying to determine what those people were going to do was like putting together a 10,000 piece puzzle. For every move, there was a counter. They also had every person in Philadelphia against me. Every eye directed toward me was met with great contemplation. I had to be able to discern intentions and positions. Some people were transparent. Their purpose was clearly punctuated by their sly, cunning smiles that conveyed possession of pertinent information regarding my situation. Others were dim-witted but subscribed to racist perspectives. Those folk were dangerous because they would become devout Sweeney loyalist to get promoted. The third kind of person were "sell-outs" the black person that had gotten to a certain level and was not about to side with an upstart, idealistic and direct young black male. They were easiest to avoid because they wanted no parts of controversy which meant they rarely spoke to me. The issue with these type of people is that they become the resident "Negro expert" and offer their slanted opinion to the person in charge. The person in charge, expectedly, accepts that opinion as gospel because that "expert" knows his or her own people and the best manner to deal with them.

Knowing all these elements exist, I had to prepare myself for the fight. This type of fight was unfamiliar. I had always played team sports which meant I always had support during any conflict. If I swung, 10 to 15 other people swung. That was a team. I was seen as an outsider now. So when Sweeney swung, he swung with the force of the administrator, ASAC, supervisor and all others that wanted to get promoted. I began to long for the support of a team and wonder why I could not be part of the DEA team. Was I wrong to want what white agents readily receive? Maybe I should have remained silent and eventually I would have been promoted. It was not that bad, I was making over $70,000. I should have just done the undercover and that would have given them less ammunition. No wonder Sweeney put me on the Met team. If I am not in the office, I cannot see what's coming. Thus I am defenseless. These thoughts haunted me during the ride home. When I pulled into the garage, frustration and the feeling of isolation forced forward tears. I sat in the car and cried, not wanting my wife to see me in that condition. Unfortunately, that feeling was masked but became part of me. I resolved to become part of the team. The main reason was to take the heat off. I began to take a more active role in group activities. I did undercover. I trained younger agents. I readily assisted the case agent (which happened to be Bob). I was trying to distance myself from turmoil.

Two months after receiving the "Warning," Sweeney called me on my cell phone. We had two way radios, so when I saw who it was, I immediately pulled to the side of the road. I expected the worse.

"Good morning, Maurice. Give me a call on the land line when you get a chance."

I drove to the nearest phone booth.

"Maurice. Yes. Just one second." He seemed to be finishing a conversation with someone. "You there, Maurice?" he said returning to the phone.

"Yeah," was the seething reply.

"I need you to call a buddy of mine from OPR (Office of Professional Conduct and Responsibility). His name is Robert Smith. He wants to ask you a few questions."

I wanted to ask about the topic but decided against it.

"Are you ready to copy the number?"

"Wait a minute", was the sharp reply. "Alright. Go ahead."

ᴧᴧ

While Sweeney recited the number, I was bombarded with an uneasy feeling that required a mental health day.

"Give him a call as soon as possible. I think he wants to schedule you for an interview." I could feel Sweeney's smile as he rejoiced in making me miserable. His voice was smug enough that saying "good-bye" before hanging up the phone was impossible. As I drove from the booth to my residence, heeding the bellowing voice that cried for me to take the day off, I attempted to squelch the rush of tears that watered my eyes. I just had to make it home. No one was there. I could let my eyes drain at home.

After that cry, I mustered the feeling to comply with Sweeney's directive. I called Robert Smith. He sounded nice enough on the phone and I immediately knew he was black. I was comforted in that fact, hoping that this process would be fair. Then I heard Sweeney's voice and the word he used to describe Robert Smith: "Buddy."

"Mr. Williamson, I would like for you to come to see me. It has been brought to our attention that you may have violated some rules and regulations. Did you speak with SAC Sweeney?" Smith asked.

"Yeah, I spoke with him and he told me to call you. That's why I called."

"Is that all he said?"

"And that you may want to interview me."

"Okay. Can you come up to Newark on Thursday?"

It was Tuesday.

"I don't see why not."

"Good. We'll schedule you for 10:00 a.m. Thursday. Just to remind you, you are not being charged with anything criminally. This is just an administrative hearing which means that no one other than you can be present."

"I can't have an attorney present?" I asked, perplexed.

ᐯᐱ

"No. Not for an administrative proceeding", Smith responded.

I thought about the voluminous violations of due process inherent in his statement, then shrugged my shoulders and shook my head. Smith then provided me with directions to his office and then we ended the conversation.

I had no personal knowledge about how OPR worked, but what I heard was enough to warrant great caution and finesse. What OPR does is gather massive information and conduct exhaustive interviews in support of intelligence it receives regarding employee misconduct. In this case, Sweeney provided "his buddy" with information and those accusations were investigated because it came from a SAC. OPR does not inform those accused of misconduct. In fact, OPR does not mention the circumstances that justify a sworn, court stegnographer recorded "deposition." They allow the person to simmer in ignorant worry knowing that will disrupt the proper conduct of one's faculties because the mind will be polluted with thoughts of 'I wonder what they have on me.' That approached succeeded in its aim when it came to me. I was immensely worried and, in my mind, unjustifiably nervous. I knew that I had attacked a SAC and this was the first orchestrated response.

When I arrived to OPR, Smith met me at the door. He did not look like he sounded. He reminded me of a Vietnam Veteran that was on the frontline and was unable to make the conversion back to "normal society." He wore an intense look on his face that his glasses could not hide. He was wound tightly. Smith introduced his senior partner, John Digravio. Digravio was a wrinkled fellow that looked to have close to thirty years on the job. I assumed he was there to view my non verbal communications.

I entered the 10 X 8 room. The first thing I noticed was

the two way mirror. I'm being recorded, I thought. The court stenographer was already in the room. Smith directed me to sit in the chair that was facing the mirror. I began having burst of regret due to the way in which I treated "bad guys." I recalled the careful placement of the person being interrogated. I vividly remembered the sense of disdain with which I viewed these people. Now I was the bad guy and with every question that feeling grew. With seasoned criminals, the investigator's questions had to be fierce and full of facts. With the new criminal, the threat of time was enough to make them divulge information. I was looking to cooperate fully, probably too fully. But the manner with which I was treated allowed for little time to focus on the truth. Just like with the real "bad guys," I had been assigned a case number and a case agent who had the necessary resources to achieve the expected result.

The interview began with a series of questions that surrounded my relationship with Mike, the snitch.

"Mr. Williamson, when did you establish the informant what measures did you take to ensure his safety? Before you answer that, you were aware that he was in fear of his safety?"

I looked at Smith with an expression of sheer confusion and bewilderment. My mind remained stuck in the fact that I was the subject of an OPR investigation. No matter how I tried to convince myself, I began to feel like a criminal. I was bad guy, exactly how they wanted me to feel. The battle between what I knew happened and what they wanted me to say raged like a stubborn fire. I anticipated the sequence of questioning, contemplated my responses and made deliberate eye contact while suspended in deleterious thought about the real reason I was here. I should not have been here. I just wanted to get promoted. I had too much going on.

After a series of introductory questions, Smith reached the crux of the matter.

"Did you or did you not instruct the informant to provide less than truthful information to DEA management?" Smith jabbed like a veteran boxer.

That's a no brainer, I thought. "No, I did not", I responded.

"We have an affidavit from the informant where he says that you told him to lie to DEA management because they were out to get you. We also have statements from your IRS partner where she states that you asked her to ask the informant to be less than truthful. Is that true?"

My confusion was growing exponentially and anger began to seep through.

"I already told you I did not tell him to lie about anything."

"We also have a telephone conversation between you and the informant dated May, 25. Would you like to discuss it?"

Oh, shit. Had I become a kingpin drug dealer that leased the streets to prostitutes and the like for illegal gain? Had I sank to the highest level of criminal activity where wire tapping was necessary? And to use that snitch, that four time convicted felon snitch, and take him at his word so that OPR could initiate an investigation against me was insane. They controlled the dice, however. They had all the statements, conducted all the interviews and had every piece of paper they wanted. I was not privy to any of this information.

"Yeah, lets discuss it", I said attempting to mask my anger. This was one time I was glad I was black for if I were white, I would have been red as a beet and they would have known I was about to explode.

"The informant stated that you told him during that conversation to be less than tRoseful with DEA management. He gave a sworn statement to that effect. Your IRS counterpart also provided a statement that you provided her with information that you wanted her to relay to the informant that was less than truthful. Why would they say this?"

That's a good damn question, I thought. Why would they give me up?

"Let's go at it this way. Did you ever have discussions with you IRS counterpart about the informant and what he would say to DEA management and what he should say to DEA management?"

"If you're asking me if I told her to tell him to lie about something, the answer is no, I did not."

That was not enough for Smith. I observed frustration sprouting from his face.

"We're going to take a ten minute break and come back. Let's go off the record", Smith said. Let me escort you to the waiting room, Mr. Williamson.", Smith continued.

I also inspected DiGravio's body language and realized that he was disappointed with the results of the interrogation thus far. He was very anxious to interject. When Smith walked me into the waiting room, I sat and immediately wanted to cry. I felt betrayed by people I thought I could trust. I felt enraged at the extent Sweeney would go to discredit my reputation. I felt helpless because I knew that despite being in the right, DEA would do everything in its power to assist a SAC in eliminating a problem. When Smith went back into the interrogation room, I felt my eyes swell and a tear fell. Despite frustrating the two ruffians, despair and I formed a bond. My reputation was ruined. In the law enforcement realm, that was everything. Before I could get to absorbed in self-pity, Smith returned to the room.

"Do you know what Giglio is?"

"Yeah", I responded from a perplexed state.

The "Giglio" Smith referred to was a federal court case involving a law enforcement officer that lied on the stand and was subsequently disallowed to testify in court because of his lack of veracity. Now I knew Smith did not believe me.

M

"Then you should act like you know." After those words, Smith just walked away as if nothing happened. I became galvanized with a calm fear that must accompany an encounter with certain death. I waited to re-enter my electric chair and face the high voltage questions from the executioners. This time there would be no reprieve, no breaks.

"We're ready for you." Smith gave a hypnotic stare that seemingly transformed my body and mind into agents to be utilized at his discretion. His eyes told me to rise and I did. His stares instructed me. I had succumbed.

I drove straight to the titty bar. I needed familiarization. Ronnie was there. I needed a friend. We talked for hours as countless pairs of breast danced in our presence. Neither of us was distracted. Ronnie listened intently as I replayed my OPR experience. He shook his head periodically which denoted his understanding of the situation.

"They always fuck with black men trying to do right," he said earnestly.

"Yeah, well, I can't take this shit no more. I'ma snap on these fuckin' crackers. But yo, dig this shit, they always get another nigger to do some of their dirty work."

My mind recalled the black face of Robert Smith. I continued my tirade.

"Fuckin' sellouts."

The courage that had been absent earlier reappeared, libations and friendship foster temerity. A familiar environment will transform timidity into comfort. I was back in my element, my zone. The conversation between Ronnie and I lasted for hours. The entire time we talked, I sensed an underlying question in Ronnie's eyes. He never asked me anything so I believed that he did not wish to infringe on my confession. I saw a drug transaction at the bar between the bartender and a patron. It was not much. I could not tell if it was weed or blow. Ronnie noticed my instinctual stare and his eyes grasped what my eyes held. He saw. When I looked back at him, he just smiled. My look was knowing, almost like Robert Smith's from earlier in the day, just not as condescending. I knew the drugs were his but I said nothing. Ronnie remained speechless; all except his acknowledgment that I knew what was going on.

"Place gets wild sometimes, dog."

How I returned to work and bore the scrutiny that Sweeney recklessly allowed to dominate my domain is still unknown. What was learned is that one person's weakness is another's opportunity. I was a walking bull's eye and everyone was throwing darts. Nothing I did would or could be proper. Sweeney made sure of that. He played the godfather and held promotion and cushy positions in abeyance until those charged with my demise (it felt like everyone) made his expectations reality. Sweeney was well on his way because the OPR interrogation had gone bad for me. I did not know how awful my OPR performance was until I saw the transcript. There, my own words damned me. I never knew the importance of an attorney until I read the transcript. I answered compound questions where any answer had the potential to be distorted. As I read, I saw my steady demise in each response, with each word I uttered. In my home, where I was reading the transcript, far removed from intimidating stares and enigmatic interrogatories being hurled like grenades, I was astounded by how I was broken.

/\/\

CHAPTER VII

/.\.\

MY FATHER HAD LEUKEMIA; advanced leukemia. The doctors prosaically recited treatment options as if memorized from a script. Chemotherapy. That was the bottom line. My father would have to undergo extensive chemotherapy to have a 20% chance of survival. My father absorbed the news with the familiar emotionless stare. My entire immediate family was in the room. Pop was always strong for us. While both my sisters, Pam and Jewell, and my mother succumbed to their emotions, my father and I remained stoic, as if somehow trying to determine the best course of action that had already been chosen for us. His eyes touched mine only briefly after his own mortality became recognized. I sensed an all consuming fear. The day betrayed the sentiments of my family. The sun boldly entered the hospital room touching everyone there.

"Well, what can you do.", my father somberly muttered so as to mask his true emotion.

No one responded. The women of my family just stared at him with wet eyes that bordered on disbelief at my father's reaction to his dire situation.

"Well, tell me, what can I do?" he said in response to the incredulous looks his women gave him. "All I can do is do

/.\.\

what the man told me to do. Y'all looking at me like I have some choices."

Those words confirmed what our earlier eye contact intimated. He was scared shitless.

"I got to do what I got to do, if I want to see my grandkids grow up."

All this time, I never made direct eye contact with my father. I used peripheral vision to study his every gesture. Every hand motion, every leg movement, every head tilting was scrutinized until I was satisfied that I knew what was going on in my father's head.

Does death make allowance for dignity, I thought? Although my father's mask was a perfect fit, the mask I was wearing was ragged and transparent. It is easier to discern other's intentions and emotions when they too are masquerading. I looked out the window at the tree that allowed the sun free reign of this room. This was not a hospital room. It was a room used for consultation or, otherwise known as the "bad news" room. I am certain that many gloomy faces accompanied by crestfallen expectations have exited its confines. The tree that captured my attention was frail and appropriately placed outside this room. My examination of the tree grew more intense. A tree's sole purpose is to provide shade, I internalized. What's with this tree? They may as well dig the thing up because it has no purpose. It can't even provide shade. Hell, it was April already and the damned thing can't make leaves.

Then my oldest sister, Jewell, began to wail. It struck me as surprising because I was consumed with my thoughts. When I turned toward her cries, she was sitting in a chair next to my father with her face buried heavily into his chest. My father instinctually embraced her and drew his chin to the top of her head. That was when a total emotional breakdown occurred. My mother and my other sister seemed to be drawn to that scene like an excited child to an amusement park. They joined in with my oldest sister and the one cry became a chorus of mournful sentiment for all to hear. They surrounded my father and hugged him in unison. I stood passionless watching the display of raw emotion, unable to bring myself to tears or empathize with my female kin. My older sister glanced at me with an expectant look that was magnified by her wet eyes, just as the sun's heat is increased through glass. She wanted me to come over and join the family only, pre-funeral exhibition. I could not. Her eyes remained fixed on me until she returned to my father's chest. No one else even looked at me. Did they know I was wearing a mask? My father waited until absolutely necessary to begin chemotherapy.

A day after his first round of chemotherapy, sometime in October, I went to visit my father. This time, he was in a room that had no trees to see, only the Philadelphia sky line. The sun could not make its presence felt to the complete room. My father's bed remained just out of reach. There, under the glow of manufactured lighting, my father lay. The many contraptions by his bedside were intimidating. Each beep and air compression seemed to be an ominous signal of impending death. As my father attempted to open his eyes, he blinked incessantly. He was trying to re-enter the world chemotherapy kidnapped from him. It became obvious that the chemotherapy drugs allowed him temporary refuge in our world.

"Hey, man," he said with his voice still raspy from the rigors of chemical warfare. "How long you been here?"

He motioned for me to hand him the bed remote control so that he could lay upright. Somehow, the device was knocked off the bed and it dangled just inches from the floor like a man being hung.

M

"Here you go, Pop. You know how to work this thing, right?"

His eyes answered the question sarcastically.

"So how you feelin', Pop?"

"I get a blood transfusion later this evening. I'll be feeling better after that. Should be home soon. How the kids doing?"

I could not tell him that they were not coming to see him. I did not want my young daughters so intimately aware of death, not yet.

"They're fine."

"You know Michele came to see me before the first chemo."

I raised my eyebrow but I should have known. I had no control of my professional or personal life. My brow returned to its original, stoic position.

"She did, huh. It must have slipped her mind."

"Maurice, don't screw up your marriage. You got a good girl."

His voice and eyes pleaded with me to alter my life, to realize and accept my blessings. I was stuck in selfish depression and blinded by megalomania. I became cognizant at that moment that my life and my job situation was my all consuming endeavor. I knew I was going to be fired soon. I could feel it. But no one seemed to understand. I was fighting a winless battle against an enemy that had no remorse or tact; all results were beneficial regardless of how immorally gained. Yet, because of this man, this dying man, I was principled and maybe a bit naive. I believed that men conducted business like men. There should be no reason to lie, cheat and deceive if in the right. I wanted to expose my father for the fraud he perpetrated on me. I was an idealistic young man willing to be destroyed for a belief: Principle. I had done everything they asked me to do. Still I could not get promoted. Still I could not be completely accepted. When I challenged them and asked why, like any competent, deserving person should do, I was smacked, beat and sent toward my certain professional death. Impropriety between statements given by the CI and myself were grasped by those renegades and made to custom fit their styling like a finely altered suit. They made the word of a four time convicted felon gospel. They wanted me to admit I perjured myself. Maybe if I did, I would get away with a suspension.

"What's on your mind, Maurice? You thinking about that DEA stuff, huh?"

I barely heard my father's voice because I began a reflective trip.

Like many young men and their fathers, my father and I did not have a great relationship until I was on my own. Under his roof, I viewed him as an obdurate, uncompromising dictator. There was little space for negotiation. If a rule was violated, the subsequent punishment was swift and harsh. At least for me. My older sisters never met my father's belt. They were girls and, as it appeared to me, the world seemed kinder for them. For me, however, the world was a harsh reality of law and punishment. I try to count the number of times a leather belt transformed my childhood into a horrific state of trepidation. I remember the slave-like beatings I would receive from my father. What I remember most was the feeling of detachment, fear and grave anxiety as I waited for my father to come home after being suspended from school. My sisters remember that the neighborhood became oblivious to the screams that forced their way through the window and into the early evening air.

My father often had migraine headaches. If by happenstance I was not receiving his form of corporal punishment, he would drop his briefcase in the dining room, ascend the stairs, enter his bedroom, close the shades and lay fully dressed in the bed. No one would enter the room. This, like my juvenile indiscretions, occurred frequently. My father, after I moved and began working, began disclosing the mystery surrounding his "dark room." Today, he revealed all.

"You know, Maurice, I used to go to my room and cry."

That confession was indirectly solicited because my father knew of the troubles I was having at work. He listened intently to me, as if waiting for me to exhibit wisdom his words and actions had equipped me with. Of course, words of wisdom are lost on the inattentive young and not found again until time of turmoil.

"Why?"

Not only did my father have frequent migraines, he also suffered from hypertension. Forgetting all his health ailments and afflictions, my father was and is an icon of strength. His athletic frame, deep dark complexion and baritone voice was an indication to the world of his physical prowess. His confidence, inflated by his college education, was surely intimidating to whites. To my way of thinking, there was nothing that would make my father cry. So, perplexed, I heard his declaration of weakness. I awaited justification.

"Man, when I was at Rohm and Haas, a white supervisor of mine yelled at me in front of my co-workers about something he thought I didn't do."

Immediately, I was in awe of that white man. He yelled at my father? Courage of that sort is typically reserved for people like Spartacus or those who were fighting with a purpose against oppression. Not those wishing to exhibit a degree of superiority. As my father continued the story, I waited for the part where he grabbed this white man and choked the life out of him.

"It took everything in me to keep from knocking his head off. But what I did was go to his office later that day and tell him that if he ever reprimanded me in public again, I was going to 'take appropriate recourse."

I am sure that man knew what my father meant. His stare would force a standing man to sway as if struck by a powerful wind. His stare also left little speculation as to his intentions.

"After that, I remember training another white guy on how to do the job. Six months later, he was my supervisor."

My father massaged his forehead with his fingers. The IV lines and other attachments to his body made that motion appear as if it were being controlled by a puppeteer. He still fought to understand why he was not promoted. Almost twenty-five years later, he still was baffled. He did not wear the scar of discrimination openly. In fact, I believe he wished he could forget. However, when I began to tell him of my frustrations in dealing with whites on the job, he wanted me to realize that nothing much has changed. For close to ten minutes, my father recalled with disturbing clarity incidents of racial discrimination in the work place. The more he spoke, the more I realized I was not an isolated case. That is, educated black men have been bludgeoned for years. This invariably led to a debate on whether or not it was better to be a black man then, during my father's time or now, during my time.

We first agreed that it was not advantageous to be black in his day or mine. Two or three hundred years of repeated ignorance and perpetuated negative perception is a difficult if not impossible doctrine to abandon. My father, being a man of experience, spoke first on the topic. Before he began, his delight at being able to share ordeals with his son consumed him. To the liquor cabinet he went. After pouring two drinks, he sat on the coach and swirled the ice in his glass with his finger.

"Would you have been able to take it if a white guy at your job called you a nigger?"

"They do it anyway, just not to my face."

"That's not the question. The question is would you be able to handle it? See, I had three children and a wife. I couldn't just come home one day unemployed."

I looked away from my father and raised my eyebrows. It surprised me how tolerant he was with the white man and how rigid he was with me. I wanted to ask how he could work in that environment. But he made it clear it was for the family.

"Well, Pop. At least you knew where they were coming from. None of this smile in your face stuff. You had to respect their honesty. Nowadays, you can't tell what a white guy is thinking. You have to be a lot more aware. To me, that is more stressful and discouraging than a white guy that just out and out calls me a nigger. I know what to expect from him. I don't know what to expect from the other ones."

My father shook his head in an understanding manner possibly surmising that agreeing with me, since I had his stubbornness, would help the conversation continue. Or maybe he did comprehend that unsuspecting discrimination was the worst kind. We had finished our first drink and my father instinctively took both glasses to his bar for a refill. He came back, handed me a fresh glass of cognac and began to speak.

"I understand that. But that don't change a damn thing. The white man is telling you the same thing he was telling me. The problem is you, and I mean people your age, think that you really have a chance to do something. They will only let you go as far as they want you to go. And people like you, they fear. They can't stand to see a young black man do anything positive. They definitely didn't want you to call them on their wrongdoings. When you do, they will destroy you. You can't act as if you know it all either."

"They do."

"That don't matter. If you know it all or think you know it all, what can they teach you? Nothing. If you don't need them, you are a threat. If you can do a good job without them, they will try to do something to mess it up. You have an air about you that says 'you don't need anybody'. You better change it or your problems will get worse."

"Hold up, Pop. Why do I have to change anything? I do my job well. They even say I do my job well. I can't change what I am. I work harder than them and longer than them. I'm doing my job."

My father shook his head again. This time, however, it was not an assenting nod. This time his face wore a look of extreme disbelief. His look was reminiscent of his expressions of cynicism that accompanied one of my childhood lies. Then, without changing his face, my father's life experience came forward.

"You do know you're black don't you?"

My father spoke as if he believed that I somehow became homogenized, as if I had forgotten that I was black.

"That's the danger of education. You all think that affords you unlimited opportunity. In a way it does. It gives you what you need to compete. But then you begin using it, people become threatened. You know those people that have been with a company for 15, 20 years? They don't want change. They just want you to come in and go with the flow. They want you to be happy where you are. If you start bucking the system or question it, you're going to have problems. And if you're black and buck the system, you won't be there long. Haven't you seen it yet? Somebody like you, if you were white, would be the greatest thing since sliced bread. They would say, 'That guy sure is aggressive. He's doing a hell of a job.' But because you're black, you're a problem. The problem is not that you're a problem, it's that you're black."

When you hear a figure you celebrate as being strong and steadfast, that raised you to believe that right is right and wrong is just that, when you hear him lament that the world is not fair, and you know his complaints are justified, the quixotic, idealistic perspective education and ambition fosters is destroyed. The equal opportunity speeches from our politicians become empty words.

"If what you're saying is right, then why even try? Why beat my head against a wall?"

My father taught me that hard work will be rewarded. I believed that. Now he was asking that I adopt a pessimistic attitude towards my ability to achieve. My father was saying that being black is a handicap that is rarely overcome. His candid statements revealed unrealized achievements.

"You deal with this stuff for your children and hope, by some miracle, that things change and everyone gets a fair shake."

I understood why whites loved Martin Luther King, Jr and feared Malcolm X. The 'I Have a Dream" speech spoke of hope for our children. The 'Indictment of the White man' speech spoke of changes now. Martin believed in non-violence while Malcolm believed in striking back. My father, apparently embracing both ideals, endured the 1960's, 1970's and 1980's so that I could get a college education, like him, and better opportunities. So that I could "strike back" for him. Yet, for all his effort and due diligence, the same barriers my father encountered are identical to those I face. For all the rhetoric, marches and demonstrations protesting for societal revisions and the subsequent "civil rights laws" of the 1960's, being Black remains a liability. Discrimination and ignorance formed a bond with the "radical" and "agreeable" sects of the underprivileged and under represented to create the perception of change.

Our political conversation concluded. We began to discuss sports, our favorite topic. I knew that life was not fair.

/\/\

But whose fault is it that I believed hard work and a steadfast belief in right and wrong would propel me through mainstream society? I cannot blame society. I can only blame the man that raised me.

I returned from my journey and my father had drifted off to sleep. The same man that lay near death was selfless enough to share his words of experience while full of life and even now. I left feeling embarrassed and learned. I would have to shed both on the drive home. I had to work tomorrow. I had to embrace reality.

CHAPTER VIII

/.\

REALITY WAS A DIFFICULT PROPOSITION THOSE DAYS. Even though the recollection of my conversation with my father was insightful, it was not enough to prevent a total relapse into the abyss of self pity. Oh, how difficult to mold his words into action, I thought. With each stare from those people in the office, that crew to which everyone seemed to belong, I felt the need to issue harsh retaliation. How was one to operate under such scrutiny? If I tried to work, my effort was derailed by Sweeney's clones. If I did not attempt to work, my disinterest was recorded and taken to be incompetence.

Three days after visiting my father in the hospital, DEA's propaganda against me began to reap rewards. I began to question myself, my actions and my suitability to be a special agent in their elite organization. I began to believe what Steve wrote about me. The sly whispers from those enjoying my demise grew louder, to the point of boisterous. Then the moment they all wanted, like finally being able to indulge in sexual escapades with a fantasy, came to fruition.

I was called to Sanchez's office. The ominous cloud that grew daily finally relented to the Sweeney assault and completely covered my sun. On the way to his office, my head was

/.\

bent as if I had noticed something different about the office floor. I tried to muster smiles for those who wished me well, the black support staff. For everyone else, it was a smile of defiance. Steve happened to be leaving the front office as I was entering. He sped away as if his nightmare had just been realized. Such a fucking punk, I thought. I noticed that Sweeney was in his office. So why was it that Sanchez was doing this deed? This was the coup de gras, the final chapter of this criminal conspiracy and the kingpin did not want to see my face? I did not understand. Fucking punk, I thought to myself. Sanchez motioned me into his office. Before I could sit down, he placed a letter from the disciplinary board before me.

"Read this," he said with the smirk of an aloof winner.

It read as follows:

"Mr. Williamson, this is to advise you that you are being placed on paid administrative leave with the intent to terminate your employment with DEA."

There were several more paragraphs but I could not read any further. All that I was, that confident, brash and assertive young man sank to realms unknown. The 180 degree turn was made, completely.

"You can pack up what you need and Bob Rogers will give you a ride home." His callousness crushed me even further.

"I'll be back later to pick up your gun and badge."

I looked up from my floor inspection and noticed that he did not appear as pompous as his words sounded. Shock and surprise did not allow any movement. Embarrassment ensured that my departure from this great disappointment from this office would be sloth-like. Another great change occurred: I realized how much of a man my father was to endure.

When I finally stood, my legs felt as if I was in the final 100 of a 1/4 mile, the infamous last turn. I entered his office defiantly. I left passively. As I left the front office, I looked to my left, towards Sweeney's office. Devoid of any thought and with nothing to lose, instinct lured me to his office. Suddenly, my father's voice rang in my head. "Don't make a bad situation worse." So there, at the door to Sweeney's office, where I could hear him on the phone, I stopped. I stopped as the secretaries watched in anticipation. I turned abruptly and walked at a quick pace away from my torturer. I went to my desk and began to gather personal belongings. Finally, confusion, despair and frustration bore tears. The tears would not stop despite my effort. There, in front of other grown men and women, I cried. Not one word was spoken. In fact, my soon to be former co-workers left the office one by one as if they were elementary school kids coming in from recess. Bob was the only one that remained. He pulled me into the supervisor's office.

"What happened?" he said with a truly sympathetic tone.

I first offered the "what do you think happened look." Bob had supported me from day one. No need to be angry with him. I swallowed and spoke between tears.

"They put me on admin leave with the intent to fire."

I looked straight into his eyes and he appeared to be in a greater state of disbelief than I. As tear after tear trickled toward my chin, Bob left his seat and hugged me. I cried uncontrollably on his shoulder. I consciously attempted to rebuke the feeling of emasculation to no avail. It was an unfamiliar visitor in my realm, an unwelcome guest that they created. I had been completely and utterly defeated and all that remained was a man's shoulder that served as the only obstacle to utter insanity. His shoulder proved to be a formidable obstruction to and emancipator of current emotions. My tears soaked my face and provided all an outward symbol of my internal distress. After the leakage ceased, the evidence of my turmoil remained. I went back to packing boxes with a white trail on my face that stretched from my eyes to my jaw.

ᴧᴧ

Bob had always championed my cause. He knew, as did the entire office, that I deserved to be promoted. The phone rang and Bob answered it.

"I'll be right there", I heard him utter in monotone.

"Maurice, I have to go up front to meet with Sanchez. Don't go anywhere until I get back. It'll be alright, man."

He gave me a manly pat on the shoulder that hid compassion. I returned an acknowledging grin that fell just short of a smile. When he left to go meet with Sanchez, I continued my packing. There was no one else in the group so I cussed and cried without concern while packing pictures of smiling faces surrounded by large seizures of narcotics. I packed letters of commendation that were sent by various agencies acknowledging my outstanding performance. I packed pictures of my daughters that I had in cheap plastic frames upon my desk. When I looked at their smiling eyes I cried. I had endured much to arrive at a financial state where I could provide for them. They, those bastards, were taking that from me. My children would not care that I took a stand based on principle, the same principles I try to instill in them. My father is a smart man, I thought.

I just completed one box when Bob came back in the group.

"Maurice, they want me to take you home and take your gun."

To law enforcement people, to have your gun and badge taken is a disgrace. But in this case, to have my only friend in this office be made responsible for the collection of these items was mentally debilitating.

CHAPTER IX

⋀

So I went back to my familiar. Ronnie was there and I needed his shoulder. One after another, I consumed cognac from the snifter. Ronnie watched me waiting for a burst of guileless confession.

"I don't believe this shit, dog. I been with them mother-fuckers for what, a fuckin' seven, eight years and this is how they do me. I can't believe this shit, man."

I spoke to Ronnie as if he knew my situation when he was oblivious. He recognized there was a problem but he was not aware what the problem was.

"What happened, man", he asked with a genuine stare.

"I'm going to get fired", I said emotionless. As I stared at nothing, I vaguely heard a pulsating bass line screaming the rhythm of the hip hop classic "Five Minutes of Funk." That song temporarily dissipated my cloud of despair and frustration and forced a head bobbing that told the world I had no problems.

"They gonna fire you?"

"Yeah. They put me on leave with pay until they fire me."

"Leave with pay. When this shit happen?"

"Today. A couple hours ago."

⋀

"That's fucked up but at least they paying you."

How he extracted a glimmer of positive light from my seemingly hopeless situation was extraordinary. I laughed mockingly at his comment. His face remained serious.

"I'm serious, dog. At least you got money coming in. You'll be alright. How's Pop?"

His concern for my father caused an abrupt conclusion to my rhythmic pleasure. I began to cry.

"He's real sick. Real sick." I stammered trying to regain my composure. I looked toward Ronnie so that he could feel the urgency of my father's situation. Ronnie's face became solemn. I think he understood that I was at the brink of what is humanly tolerable. He grabbed the back of my neck but did not speak.

"Hey, sweetie. Get him whatever he wants. Whatever, alright?" Ronnie said to the bartender.

She responded affirmatively between a brief stare that attempted to determine why Ronnie was being so generous.

"If you need to crash at the crib, let me know. The kids alright?"

I shook my head yes.

"Cool. Let me handle something real quick and I'll be back."

I knew what he had to handle.

"I ain't going nowhere. Handle what you got to handle."

Ronnie left his seat and went into the back.

"Let me get a henny and coke", I asked the bartender.

"No problem, sweetie."

CHAPTER X

/\.V.\

WHEN I WOKE UP THE NEXT MORNING, my wife and kids had already left the house. She had no idea that I was on administrative leave. She probably thought that I just had one of those nights. There seemed to be an excessive amount of post-drunk paste in my mouth. I hit the listerine bottle hard. I had a pulsating pounding in my head that only allowed me time to rinse my mouth, urinate and return to bed. I was thirsty but had to sleep it off. My wife probably thought I was an alcoholic. Maybe I was. She had not said much to me for awhile. I think because I was too swollen with shame to bother her or the kids. I was lost in myself. I could not recall the last time we had sex. We would periodically talk about the kids, their activities and such. That was it. I grew accustomed to her acting as if I did not exist, how she would put eggs on everyone's plate but leave mine in the pan, how she would watch T.V. upstairs while I was in the family room, how she would walk past me in the hall without so much as eye contact. It was a battle of wills. My wife is a stubborn woman. I am a stubborn man. I adopted an "I don't give a fuck" attitude that manifested itself when she refused my sexual advancements. I said on more than one occasion to my wife that if she did not deal with my needs, I would get them satisfied else

/\.V.\

where. She was not moved. So I acted on my most primal needs seeking and finding reckless pleasure. She never asked any questions. That deflated the joy of cheating. I began regularly coming home 3 or 4 in the morning without offering an explanation. When I entered the bed with the motley aroma of alcohol, smoke and female perfume, she appeared sound asleep and made no comments.

It is futile to trace our issues to its root. It just happened. I do not know if it was lack of sex, lack of adventure or fear of commitment, but our love and marriage disintegrated as rapidly. My job situation and my self-pity did not help our relationship. It further magnified my need to be alone or so I thought. We lived with each other for our children. We were careful not to appear as two individuals in front of them.

When we first began dating, I was in control. I dictated the time and location we would meet. She did not mind. She was unemployed and waiting for her Pennsylvania Bar Test results. She was insatiable. I was cool. I had a G-car (Black tinted Mustang), a gun, federal credentials and supreme confidence. I had just purchased a town house in a Philly suburb. The bachelor's crib. I treated the house like such by parading girl after girl through there. She was the only one that would cook, though. So, very subtly, she maneuvered herself into a position where she became a fixture at my crib. We became friends. I carried her to the all important meet the mother meeting. My sister was there also. Everyone seemed to get along and that eased the idea that she was infringing on my bachelorhood. Seven months later, and after a several melodramatic relationship severing episodes, she became pregnant.

My mother did not like it. My sister, Pamela, despised her pregnancy.

"That girl trapped your dumb ass!" she said without remorse.

When I thought about it while there was a huge gulf in our

relationship, that did appear to be the case. I had a good job, a car, a gun and a badge. I never pondered her intentions during Jordyn's conception and birth. I was just be happy that she was having my child. My father was ecstatic at the thought of another boy in the fold. He embraced her and her pregnancy with a pleasant perspective. I wrapped myself around his joy and my pride, hoping he was right. I did resolve to myself that I would not, for any reason, abandon this child. I was going to be the most responsible father humanly possible.

I bribed Ronnie with KFC and Henieken to help me paint the baby's room. A palpable feeling of anachronism dominated my psyche and instinct whenever I was around Ronnie. I knew he was a felon (he had prior narcotics charges) and I knew he liked to smoke weed. Fortunately, he never put me in a precarious environment where I would have to choose friendship or employment. She did not like him. The reasons were never clearly stated why she adopted and nurtured a spiral of discontent towards Ronnie. We all were raised in the same community. His type was well represented. I always thought he had some dirt on her that she did not want disclosed. Ronnie never let me know if he had any disparaging information. He never spoke negatively about her despite knowing his devalued status in her mind.

Anyway, Michele and I had a solid relationship that got stronger as my daughter Jordyn got older. That circumstance led to the birth of my second daughter, Lindsay. As if she were a director deftly foreshadowing her intentions, her interest in family began to wane. Her profession (an attorney) became her obsession. She seemed to be consumed by other's perspectives and opinions of her work ethic rather than caring for her children and husband. Not only did that place great restraints on my career aspirations but someone had to be home with the kids. It dominated our conversations. Those conversations grew from controlled frustration to unbridled emotional tirades capable of waking the kids. I still loved her, but this was not in the contract. For more than three years, I felt like a single parent. I would carry the girls to daycare and offer explanation after explanation as to why I also had to pick them up. I had the benefit of freedom that, if I had another job, would not exist. So I tempered my outburst towards my wife with a supreme feeling of accomplishment. I could take care of my kids alone. A mother was not a prerequisite for this family. Yet, to the world, I always presented her in a manner appropriate for a consummate mother and spouse. When people would speak favorably about my wife, I would cringe in an attempt to subdue my true opinion of my wife. My father still was her greatest advocate. I would listen, ad nausea, to how great she was and how lucky I was. I was fortunate because I had two beautiful girls, not because of her. Then it happened. All the late hours, the missed trips to the zoo, the damn near abstinence we had been practicing for the past nine months, it revealed itself during a sleep induced murmur. What was keeping her from her family, what was keeping her from this house, was answered as she slept one spring night. She came in "beat" from a day's work. She was always tired. She kissed the girls that I had bathed and put in bed, then meandered to the shower oblivious to the notion that I was searching for a real explanation. This was her routine. It was 11:00 p.m. I was always bringing case related materials home. I was always awake when she arrived, hoping for a dramatic shift in her interest. There never was.

After she showered, if she was in a good mood, she would say "goodnight." She was in a positive emotional state the night all was revealed. When she uttered "goodnight", it was followed by a sigh of satisfaction that originated deep in her soul and expressed a pleasure which I had not manufactured. I said nothing as she fell quickly into a heavy, contented sleep.

M

Hell, I might as well try my luck, I thought to myself. So I began to caress her back and touch just the smallest part of her breast that was not veiled by her arm. As I began to reach for her nipple, she uttered, "Not now, Jerome."

What did she say? Wait a minute, what did she say? I know she did not say Jerome, I thought to myself, treading perilously in the deep waters of deception and confusion. I heard what the hell she said. That bitch said Jerome. My name ain't fuckin' Jerome. I ought to shoot this bitch right now. I know she's the fuck awake. She's just laying there because she knows she just fucked up. She needs to lay there to figure out how the fuck to explain this. I know that bitch can feel my stare.

By now, I was sitting in the bed against the headboard and she had not flinched. Her back was facing me. Even though her body lay perfectly still, it seemed to ridicule me knowingly. From her earlier uncontrollable sigh of satisfaction to her involuntary admission, all but her mouth was seemingly smiling having totally humiliated me. I said nothing. I did nothing. I pondered everything. I left the bedroom a defeated man sentenced to knowing yet never sharing the excruciating torment caused by my wife's tacit admission of infidelity. I never mentioned it to her, what she said that night. I believe we both played dumb.

I grew exceedingly indifferent to her late nights. In fact, when she came home, I left. Sometimes I just hung with the fellows. Sometimes I spent the night with female friends. I made sure that I was home before my girls woke up. She was not amused by my exploits but never asked any questions. We both knew what was going on. I knew she was aware of what I was doing. That is exactly what I wanted. However, she never exhibited the pain that deceit causes. I saw no signs. When my job problems worsened, I had no intention of sharing it with her. We had grown apart and the gulf was too wide to be rectified.

ᴍ

(HAPTER XI

/.V.\

JUST THE OTHER DAY, MY FATHER AND I HAD BREAKFAST. He was trying to console me regarding my termination. His first bout of chemotherapy went well but he had to continue to go to the doctor for transfusions. His condition plummeted quickly. He, in a matter days, went from the restaurant to barely conscience and permanent residency in the hospital.

"Hey, Pop. What's up? I know I haven't been here in a minute but this job thing is eating my mind. They are definitely out to get me. Maybe I should learn to keep my mouth shut, like you said. Anyway, how are you today?" I said to my motionless father deep into a coma induced sleep. E had slipped into a coma three days ago. Self pity and fear, fear of seeing a man I idolized as a pillar of strength meeting his demise, kept me from his bed side. My mother stuck her head in the room.

"Maurice. The doctor wants to see us now."

"Okay mom," I responded. "Pop, I'll be right back. Gotta go talk, well listen, to your doctor. Be right back."

On this cold winter's day in late December, we were all assembled in the room: Mother, Jewell and Pam, Michele and me. Daylight savings time made 4:45 P.M. appear like midnight.

/.V.\

The glass allowed the crescent moon to peer into the room. The doctor spoke in a tone absent sympathy.

"Your father and husband has gone into respiratory failure. The only thing keeping him alive are those machines right now. I'm not sure how long you want him to remain on these machines. That is why I have called you here. His chances of survival are non-existent. Once we turn the machine off, he will go into heart failure and pass away. What we can do to ease his transition is give him a heavy dose of morphine. That will ease any discomfort he has as he makes his transition. Do you have any questions?"

While everyone digested what the doctor stated, I aimlessly looked through the window, at the crescent moon for answers.

"Can he hear us?" I asked.

"Yes he can", the doctor responded.

"Then let's say goodbye y'all." I said in a solemn yet exacting tone.

"Doctor", I continued, "we're going to say goodbye then we'll reach out to you when it is time. We won't be that long."

"Take all the time you need", he said. Then we all stood and left that room to go say goodbye.

Michele grabbed my hand. When we entered the room, she was the first to kiss my father's cheek and say goodbye. She immediately left the room. When she left, a nurse came in timidly.

"I just wanted to give him his morphine. Is that okay?"

As my sisters stared with disgust at having a family moment interrupted by outsiders, I told her to proceed with her duties.

"Should I turn the machine off?" she asked sheepishly.

I nodded affirmatively. The nurse turned the machine off

M

and said, "Goodbye, Mr. Williamson." Then she left the room. A tear trickled down the left side of my father's face. He knew he was dying and I could not imagine being him, knowing it was over.

My mother called on me to perform the most difficult task: contacting the undertaker. Ambivalence cornered my emotions and played the uncongenial emotional host as I dealt with the task at hand. I wanted to cry and have a demoniacal emotional meltdown.

"Ah, yeah. We're going to need you down here. My Pop just passed away." As I listened to myself speak, I was amazed that my voice and demeanor so greatly contradicted my soul.

"We'll be there shortly."

After I relayed the information, the phone slipped out my hands and onto the hook. I looked around at my sisters and mother. My mother always dealt with matters, any matter, gracefully. This was no different. She did not wear the distant look I thought a wife of a recently deceased spouse should have. If she were thinking of "the good old days", it was shielded by a calm as serene as virgin waters. My sisters were not as gracious in handling Pops death.

The funeral was well attended. My father had influenced many young men through football. He coached little league football for almost 30 years. My mother seemed relieved. For almost a week, she was bombarded by well wishers at her house. Hundreds of people came to the house, our house, my house. Their purpose was to console and ease the family's pain my father caused with his departure. To me it appeared like nothing more than hungry freeloaders wishing to satisfy culinary desires. They definitely got what they wanted.

Christmas was tough; my father's hearty laugh was silenced leaving me the heir apparent with no distinguishable qualities. It was awkward sitting in his seat and saying his prayer at the dining room table. My mother insisted on preparing dinner, and that all of us be there. My wife held my hand during the prayer. In fact, she had been nursing me since my father passed. She massaged my shoulders like she used to when we first met. We made love, passionately and affectionately, for the first time in years. She seemed to suddenly understand the intense stress caused by my father's illness and subsequent death and my job situation. No doubt, she was hurting also. However, she seemed doggedly intent on making me happy, thus giving herself a feeling of exhilaration ordinarily reserved for children playing without a care. A positive from a negative; my wife's maternal instinct, what I thought to be reserved for my off-spring, was gloriously resuscitated and served as an immediate anchor to keep me sane. It allowed me to look forward to the New Year and the expectation of better times.

My wife's friend was having a New Year's Eve party. I did not want to go but we had been doing so well for the past week that I was not inclined to deny her request. We were having my family and a few friends for our annual New Year's day short ribs and black eyed peas chow down. My wife was fine with staying for a while then coming home to bring in the New Year. The night began mildly but grew progressively festive. The host offered an array of hard liquor and good food that could not be refused. He also distributed Cuban cigars that delivered exquisite taste when chased by cognac. Dancing began and smiles were plentiful. That is all I remember. I simply blacked out from the consumption of alcohol. To this day, I do not remember how I got home. I have been drunk before, but this was my drunk plateau. I lost all sense of time and apparently, control. When I attempted to wake up on New Year's day, my drunken stupor disallowed movement. I scanned the room through the slits on my face and saw total chaos. Clothes were liberally disbursed about the bedroom furniture and on the floor. Oh shit. What did I do? My wife was not there. Every move I tried to make was countered with an involuntary need to vomit. Checkmate. I vomited on the sheets and on the bed, then on the floor. I had no control. I wished for death but settled for remaining absolutely still. The stench of the vomit suffocated the odor of alcohol that seeped through my pores. That's when I heard the door open. I heard brief conversation between two female voices. Then I heard the door being shut. The creaking of the steps made known someone was coming upstairs. I knew it was her. I felt hatred enter the room silently. I felt the stare of contempt protruding from her eyes. I viewed her image on the lacquered hon voir, carefully turning my head so as not to disturb my body. My feelings were right. Contempt was in her posture. What did I do now? Things were going so well for us. She walked towards the bathroom viewing the state of ruin. Then she spoke.

"Maurice. Do you know what you did last night?" Her voice was bold and defiant and declared the true intent of this inquiry.

I did not respond initially. I still had a raging battle between my stomach and my mind. The room was not right and when she positioned herself before me standing firm, it appeared that she was moving up and down.

"Well. Do you know what you did?"

I could not answer.

"I'll tell you what you did? You showed your entire ass last night."

I managed a groan of acknowledgment.

"You ruined the party, you fought with guests and, as if that wasn't enough, you hit me. You don't even remember, do you?"

I had no idea what she was talking about.

"I know you're going through problems but I have never seen you like this before. You drink too much. You need to stop. You hit me and that's not cool. Everyone saw you do it. How do you think that makes me look? Huh? Hell, I'm just wasting my time and energy trying to talk to you. Look at you. Sleeping in your own throw up."

If I could just speak, I would tell her how much of a whore I thought she was for cheating on me. I would have told her that I should have knocked her the fuck out for being unfaithful and being a significant portion of my downward spiral. I would have told her that she augmented my woes and was a main reason for my depressed state. However, all I could do was listen in a semi-conscious, alcohol induced stupor that would not allow rebuttal. She gave an exasperated sigh then continued.

"What are we going to do today? Do you still want people to come over?"

I gently nodded yes.

"Then you need to clean this shit up. I'll be back."

She left the room quickly and I listened to her descend the stairs. I was still drunk. I could not ask her where she was last night. I did not want to think right now. I closed my eyes.

"Boy, what is wrong with you. You got a good woman a nice family and a good job. What is wrong with you, boy? Come on, get up. Let's go get some coffee. You need some coffee."

All I could do was groan.

"Listen man, don't let them win. You letting them win. Don't let them win. You have everything anybody would want. Don't throw it all away."

The voice was very familiar but I felt my face frown in confusion. Pop?

"Don't throw it all away, man. Damn."

He was sitting on the bed right next to me. He placed his hand on my shoulder as I attempted to ease my stomach cramps by drawing up into the fetal position. When he touched me, I felt tears rush down my cheek. I could not speak. Still drunk and still immobile, I cried effortlessly. I opened my slits and realized that my downward spiral was almost complete. I also realized I was alone.

My wife called me about two weeks later. She was at work when she called. After the New Year's Eve incident, she and the kids went to her mother's house. I believe she did that so I could stew in pity with absolutely no outlet. The only escape I had was the bar and my dog, Ronnie. I often stayed at Ronnie's house since she left. Our conversations became business oriented. Ronnie's business, that is. He would ask me about the types of vehicles we used on surveillance. He would ask about how we (DEA) went about soliciting snitches and the like. He never asked about me joining him. It was coming and I had no idea what my reaction and finally, my response would be. Being on administrative leave, with pay, limits legitimate options. I could not seek other employment with that ominous OPR cloud hovering. I had to have alternatives.

My wife seemed distraught. Her "Hey", contained a depth of concern.

"What's wrong? Are the kids okay?" I asked deciphering that there was a problem.

"No, the kids are fine. Have you received any phone calls from OPR?"

"No. They haven't made a final decision yet. I'll let you know when they do." Her concerned encouraged me. Maybe we could work things out.

"Well, they called me today. A guy named Scolini. Steve Scolini. He was asking about New Year's Eve." There was a long silence. I was trying to understand how OPR found out about the incident.

"What did he say?"

"He said that they had information that you were bran-

dishing a gun and that you physically assaulted me."
Additional silence.

"Oh yeah. They also accused you of public drunkenness."

"What did you say?" I said hoping that she lied for me.

"I told them that I did not know where they got their
information, but if they called me again at my job I would sue
them for harassment. Somebody gave you up. They knew
details. Details they only could have known if they were there."

"Michele, there were only two other couples there."

"I know. So I called Margie. She said she told her mother
and that's it. Her mother does not know you even work for
DEA. Her other friends don't know who you work with."

Damn, not Jon and Kim. Why would they give me up? I
thought through the third bout of silence.

"I'm going to call Jon. I'll call you back, alright?"

"Yeah, let me know what he says. You know how I feel
about Kim. Anyway, call me back, Maurice and…don't go out
drinking."

There was that concern again. I hung up the phone with
a smile despite the situation.

"Jon, what's up. This is Maurice."

"Hey man. How are you?" He replied

"Hanging man. Hanging. Hey listen, have you or Kim
talked to anyone from DEA."

"Naw. Why, what's up?"

"What's up is that they called my wife asking about what
happened on New Year's Eve."

"No, man. We haven't spoken to anyone from DEA. How
did they find out?"

"I have no idea, that's why I'm asking you."

"I don't know what to tell you man but we didn't talk to
anyone."

"Okay, I'll get back with you soon." I then hung up the phone. He sounded genuine enough and I had absolutely no information to make a case against him and his wife. What I did know is that the information had to be filtered to Sweeney for him to forward the information to OPR. I know he had an orgasm when he received news of my New Year's Eve follies. Sweeney knew that I could not be a special agent if convicted of domestic abuse. He also knew that any negative light on him would be deflected to me if additional charges were brought against me. He was making sure I would not survive.

My wife moved back into the house shortly after being contacted by OPR. She said a unified front had to be presented to combat these new charges. My optimism grew. I began to believe our marriage would be salvaged. The kids were excited to be back home. I promised to my wife, in the kid's presence, that they would never have to leave home again. I wore the pathetic expression of a homeless person being sternly refused money. She dropped her luggage and embraced me. I was frustrated, my professional life in chaos, but for that moment, the one moment that I had everything back in my life, my life was blissful.

CHAPTER XII

MY ALTERNATIVES WERE SEVERELY LIMITED due to my eminent termination. I went to see Ronnie. I could not wait for the offer. I knew he wanted me to work for him. He knew intimate details of how I was railroaded and blackballed out of the DEA. He was one of my greatest sympathizers. He, like my father, believed that I exhibited my amassed intelligence to individuals that were not ready. I gave them too much too fast. When he came from behind the bar, he greeted me with a familiar smile that made my decision and its pending declaration that much easier. However, I still felt the need to justify my rationale, if not to assure him I was sincere, to validate and confirm my conversion.

"Hey man." Ronnie said giving me the twisted look that knowingly peered into my mind. "What's happening?"

"Ah, nothing much, dog. We need to rap", I said, staring sincerely at my glass of cognac.

"Alright. I'm listening."

"Okay. This is the deal. I'm officially fired and I need to support my kids." I turned from my glass and met his eyes. "I can help you out."

"What do you mean?" he retorted. I sensed distrust. Where was that coming from?

"You know exactly what I mean. You know this is not easy for me. Don't make it harder for me", I said with a degree of disgust that was apparent. "I know you need someone like me. And since I'm not with them, I thought I could be with you. You my man from day one. You always helped me out. Now I can help you."

Having done extensive undercover work, I recognized the frown of suspicion. What could I do to ease his fears? Despite his earlier advancements that flirted with the subject, Ronnie was taken aback by my blunt proposition. He did, however, after a stark look that suggested my death if I betrayed him, accept my proposition.

"We run it tight around here. You have to be my eyes and my conscious." His smile sealed the deal. From there we embraced and took a shot of Remy Martin. I did not want to be his conscious nor his partner in this line of work but I needed the money. What I really needed was the money to substitute for the embarrassment of being fired. Well, I wasn't fired yet, but it was my predetermined destiny as ordained by Barry Sweeney.

The shoe dropped. I had been on administrative leave for almost one year and never felt secure. In the mail I received notification that I was being terminated. I read it twice.

Its content did not change.

Dear Criminal Investigator Maurice Williamson,

Based on review of your case, Docket # 6437-0876, We find sufficient evidence to substantiate the Agency's position. Therefore, as of receipt of this letter, you are hereby terminated from your position as a criminal investigator with the Drug Enforcement Administration.

The letter also made me aware of all administrative alternatives at my disposal. They provided contact numbers and addresses if I felt it necessary to challenge this initial ruling. I knew it was coming but knowledge did not soften the impact of the letter and its words. I felt like a criminal. I was not going to fight what I perceived as a battle I could not win. They had too many resources to draw upon. They had twisted the truth to suit their needs. Their spin on events were of hurricane proportion while my spin, the truth, was but a soft spring breeze. I was left in the wake of their winds of destruction. I did not want to rebuild. I wanted to move on. Although I was being force-fed, I had to make the most of the meal. I had options. I had an option. My kids were not coming out of private school. I was not changing my standard of living. I was a highly trained investigator with intimate knowledge of how the federal system works. That skill, for whatever purpose, is highly marketable. They provided me with the skill. I was forced into its purpose.

Two weeks later, I was a part of the crew. I watched Ronnie's back like he watched mine when we were younger. His team was extensive. He had distribution points in Washington, Trenton, NJ, Wilmington, DE, and his main hub was Philly. On any day, he would unload packages from his Colombian connection worth several million. Cocaine was his narcotic of choice. Ronnie figured that cocaine was a universal drug that, if properly controlled, would evolve into what marijuana currently is: a soft drug. Ronnie trusted me with monitoring the larger transactions. After a location was set for a transaction, I would stake it out about an hour before hand. I was there to detect any suspicious activity. In particular, I was there to find any government vehicles. I knew what narcotics people drove. I also had a young woman at Philly narcotics unit that gave me information on new vehicles the narc unit received. I also had contacts with DEA (a woman) that would run extensive checks on any name I gave her. She would also give me information about new cars. Why I was most valuable to Ronnie was that I could provide him intelligence on his trade partners and workers. To be able to obtain the addresses, vehicles and prior convictions of business partners, Ronnie could make educated decisions regarding drug contacts. So, being armed with an abundance of information, knowing the names and faces of agents and state and local police undercover agents in about a four state radius, Ronnie, as was I, was certain that we could recognize a set-up. I was amazed how Ronnie's organization was allowed to act with such impunity. In less than a month, I witnessed million dollar drug transactions that forced me to reconcile with my new line of work.

I would be a star, I thought while watching several of the transactions.

I began to make suggestions to Ronnie as to how security could be tightened. I asked him to allow me to listen to negotiations so I could make a determination as to if the person was a snitch or an undercover. I knew the "code" words I told him.

"Crawl before you walk, dog", he responded.

Damn. He sounded like DEA management urging me to be complacent and patient. I did not like that type of rejection. However, he did not see my scowl of discontent.

Ronnie and I negotiated a "contract" that was very lucrative for me. I made two–three thousand a week based on the intelligence provided and deals I monitored. I made approximately nine thousand a month.

CHAPTER XIII

ΛΛ

I CAUGHT MYSELF LOOKING SQUARELY AT MY REFLECTION. I studied the eyes of this person; it seemed an unfamiliar stare shot back. What was unusual about this reflection? Who belonged to this face? I touched my eyebrow. The reflection followed suit. I tilted my head from left to right and the reflection did the same. There is nothing different, I thought. It is me and what I have become.

I then stared hard into the eyes of the person in the mirror. What did I become? I was a bright, ambitious soul consumed with career and upward mobility. I was also obsessed with the well being and security of my children. Now, almost one year after having my dreams of being a SAC in DEA brutally stripped, I was being controlled by the money and thugs that I would enjoy locking up. My soul, my true calling was in combat with reality, what I had to do. Today the feeling was more acute and seemed to open wounds that allowed daydreaming to capture my effort. I rinsed my face with cold water but the same face was there; only now it was wet. How did I let this happen to me? I was slowly being transformed into a thug that condoned without care the consumption poison. Not that long ago, I was on the street

ΛΛ

buying from this "scum" for the betterment of the community and, admittedly, professional ascension. Now I worked cooperatively with that type to ensure that narcotic transactions were consummated without obstruction. For that I was becoming wealthier than I ever fathomed. My 180 degree turn was lucrative but I had to ransom my soul.

I am not the same guy. My reflection bore that fact. Deep in my eyes, I saw a malcontent that just wanted his old job back. I missed being a "good guy." After I feverishly dried my face on the towel, seemingly trying to rid my mind and mirror of the awful, empty person that glared back at me, I realized that all change is not good. I reached a plateau but saw nothing above or beneath me. I was there alone. I had no safety mechanisms in place. It was cold and I was naked. I knew it was just a matter of time.

M

CHAPTER XV

/.V.\

SOMETHING WAS NOT RIGHT IN HIS VOICE. Ronnie sounded nervous and anxious.

"We gotta make this deal happen, dog. It's worth a lot of money", he said, while I tried to figure out what deal he was talking about.

"Let's just meet at the bar and then you can give me the 411. Not on the phone, dog", I said trying to sound disinterested.

Ronnie did not speak much, only when he was excited about something. I remember a girl named Ivy that had him talking for about one week straight. I heard the identical excitement in his voice now that I recalled when he spoke about Ivy.

We were to meet at the bar around 4:30. The bar did not officially open until 8:00. We usually had our "crew" meetings there. It was the one place Ronnie was sure the conversation could not be recorded. I arrived at the bar at 4:45. Ronnie was waiting on a bar stool holding a glass of what I believed to be cognac.

"You thirsty, man?" Ronnie asked holding a Remy Martin XO bottle. A delicate smile crept across his face. He seemed guarded.

"Yeah. Let me get a shot of that."

/\/\

I sat on the stool next to his, let the cognac burn my lips, tongue, throat and chest, then turned my body towards Ronnie.

"What the fuck is going on, man. Is everything alright? I ain't seen you like this since Ivy. You got a smile on you face and shit. Look at you."

Ronnie tried to get serious, but the mention of Ivy, the girl who pussy whipped him into submission, made him smile a recall how with amazement how much pussy used to make him do. Now his pussy was money.

"Dog", he began, "some crazy shit happen last night. I was chillin' with Hector down mira mira land, and I ran into this motherfucker named Carlos."

I was listening intently.

"Me and Carlos start talking about this and that and this motherfucker got some connects."

"What did y'all talk about?" I was the killjoy. I was the one that analyzed everything, every word and action and tried to determine the ulterior motives. I tried to recognize any threats before they became threats. That's what I was paid to do.

"We talked about this and that. Hector knows the motherfucker so he's alright. Anyway, this nigger can set us straight for about three to six months. I told you that motherfucker is Columbian."

The deal had already been set in motion. I could tell.

"Why didn't you call me, man?"

"You a fuckin' family man. This shit happen late."

"Okay. What's the deal then? What has to be done?"

"Dude said that he can drop a shipment off in New York. We have to go there and pick it up."

Then, inexplicable, Ronnie leaned toward me as if someone else was in the bar.

"We going to get 50 keys for 14K a piece."

I looked back down at my drink and thought I would rather deal with the cognac burn than the burn that was currently in my stomach. He must have been drunk when he was talking to Carlos. The price was good. That is a consequence of buying in bulk. What else had been arranged?

"Carlos is going to give me a sample tomorrow. I want you there to see if the guy is alright. If he is, we gonna make this shit happen next week."

That calmed me. But not enough.

"You just met this guy. You sure he's alright?"

"Hector said the guy is solid. Hector is solid. Said he knew him from the pen."

"What's his last name?"

"What?"

"What is this guy Carlos' last name?"

"Fuckin' Gonzales-Morales. How the fuck should I know. I didn't ask his last name." Ronnie said it with a sarcasm that questioned my suspicion.

"Okay, what was he driving?"

"He came with Hector. He had some fine honeys with him, too. Bling, bow, kaboom." Ronnie was surprisingly animated as he described the female anatomy. I knew he was to smart too be blinded by the prospect of getting laid, but I was still worried about his decision to move so quickly with this Carlos. It was unlike Ronnie to make such a drastic determination about a person without doing his homework. Since I had been with him, he relied heavily on my information to ensure his safety and keep him out of jail.

"Alright, so who's going to be there tomorrow? You gonna have Sheila get the sample from the guy?" I asked, trying to envision a location where this could go down easily.

"Naw, dog. I told Carlos to come to the bar."

"You did what?"

"Yeah. He's coming by the bar tomorrow to drop off the sample. It's cool, dog. Everything is everything."

"So what you want me to do tomorrow?"

"Whatever he comes in, try to figure out who it belongs to. See if you can follow him and see where he sleeps. Try to get some info. But I'm telling you, the boy is cool. Watch."

"With both eyes open", I responded with a caution-laced voice.

It was raining. It never seemed to rain but today, of course, it was. They had arranged a 1:00 p.m. meet time. I was on location at 12:15. I sat in my car, gripping the steering wheel like I wanted to grip Ronnie's throat. This is too fast, I thought, while ignoring Pattie Jackson from WDAS, on the radio. I searched the side and rearview mirrors for this Carlos. The general description Ronnie gave me was, 'Oh yeah, dog. He's about 5'10", dark hair, you know how them motherfuckers look'. That was enigmatic so I was hunting for a fancy car. Sure enough, at about 12:50, a new Hummer, with rims that had to be 22", pulled up in front of the bar. The driver had to be Carlos. He had to be. He was wearing a khaki colored trench coat and dark pants. I was parked about fifty yards from the bar but I could easily see his rings that donned huge diamonds. Surprisingly, he was alone. That eased my concern. He walked into the bar empty handed with a swagger that screamed confidence, maybe too much confident.

He was alone. No tail, no protection. I moved from my location and squared the block. I saw no one. There were no windshield wipers operating on parked cars. That was an extraordinary exhibition of trust. But there was no money involved so I guess Carlos was not threatened.

I immediately called my contact so I could run his tags. My girl from Philly P.D. was not available. She was "out on the street" I was told. I called my contact from DEA and got her answering machine. A very uneasy, gnawing feeling returned. I wrote down the tag with the intent of running it later. More clouds rolled in and the rain intensified. I parked my car again and relaxed my neck by lying back on the headrest. Be glad when this is over, I thought.

Shiela was the only one in the bar. She had no money but she was always armed. Her sole purpose was to get the ounce sample and then call me. After I received the call, I was to call Ronnie and let him know everything was fine.

I picked my head up to regain a visual on the front of the bar. Carlos was exiting. I snapped picture after picture while he walked to his vehicle. I wanted a face to go with the rest of his information. My cell phone rang. It was Shiela. She wanted me to come inside so that the "stuff" could be tested. She did not want to do it alone, furthering the parallel between the "good and bad guys." We too never logged evidence, counted money or transported drugs alone. Chain of custody is a very important thing at DEA. Everything had to be witnessed.

I gave Ronnie a call to let him know that Shiela had the sample. I asked him if he wanted me to go inside the bar. Ronnie said I should.

"Don't see no harm in that," he said.

As I exited my vehicle and opened my umbrella, I noticed that Carlos' truck did not move. I continued towards the bar. Carlos flashed his high beams three times. Just then, the eerie, uneasy feelings that I had for two days became a full blown reality. I stopped no more than ten feet from his truck knowing I had nowhere to run. As I was cuffed by former coworkers, I lost myself in contemplation. Who the hell set me up this time?

Shiela was dragged from the bar. While being held by the

arm, she looked at me. Her eyes labeled me a snitch. She may have been wondering why I did not know this was a sting operation. It was my job to know.

The ride to the federal building was a familiar one. It conjured memories of times when I was the one laughing at the "idiots" in the back seat. Didn't they know they would get caught eventually? I thought. Why did I think myself smarter than those I locked up?

/\/\

CHAPTER XVI

⋀

THIS IS WHAT IT CAME TO: I was being questioned by former coworkers for being a member of a criminal enterprise; allegedly. I knew the routine so I calmly sat masking the internal screams for help. When the door opened, I glanced toward the moaning hinges from behind a round table. The blue plastic chair and the congestion of the small room were growing unbearable. A familiar face, even in this situation, relaxed me.

"What's up, man? Fucks going on here?" questioned Steve Scolini, Assistant Special Agent in Charge for the Philadelphia Field Division.

I was amazed that he was now the ASAC. Just 15 months ago, he was my supervisor. Seven months ago, he was asking me and my wife about New Year's eve as an OPR investigator. Now, he was an ASAC. Why couldn't that be me?

"Your boys got the wrong one, as usual. Do you still send your people to fuck with me, even after all the shit I've been through?" I asked, defiantly.

A smile crept across Steve's face as I sat speechless, amazed at Steve's gall. Hundreds of times, I infiltrated organizations and was responsible for the demise of many drug dealers and murderers. The recognition for arrest and seizures went to the case agents. I was never a case agent. When I was, my thunder was stolen.

"This is some silly shit you're in. Listen, because I know you know the game, just tell me what you did and we'll talk to the AUSA and see what we can do."

"Do I look like my head screws the fuck on and off? I'll wait for my Jew boy because you know how you motherfuckers are. Y'all like to make up shit."

Steve smiled like a wayward husband in a Chinese massage parlor. I was not sure if he was irate or sympathetic.

"What is this about, man? Didn't you ruin me enough the first time?" I asked

"You ruined yourself", Steve replied sharply. "You lied, got caught and that was that."

"You and I both know that's bullshit." I adjusted my posture. "Y'all went after me because…"

The hinges moaned again. Tracey Roberts, the assistant United States Attorney, entered timidly. She had worked this investigation from its inception and would have excused herself if she believed that I was involved. She and I worked cases together and it was not known that Tracey was party to an adulterous affair with me. I was not married at the time and I lusted after Tracey because she was an exceptional pretty older white woman. I often teased Tracey during our furtive interludes that white women her age usually resembled albino prunes. Tracey never was offended, maybe because she was beautiful. She had not seen me since I went on administrative leave. She wished to avoid any hint of impropriety. Being associated with a convicted "liar" would severely injure her career, even though it was almost complete.

"Bringing out the heavy hitters on this one, huh, Steve?" I watched Steve's lack of reaction then addressed Tracey.

"Hello, Ms. United States Attorney. Looking good as usual."

"Maurice", Tracey responded with a nod and a seemingly uncaring intonation. "What's going on here?"

"Same shit that was going on before."

While Steve was my supervisor, I started an investigation based on information I received from an individual I arrested. Steve never trusted the snitch and discouraged me from establishing him as an informant. The snitch was dirty. I knew that. But I wanted to make a case for myself, not for others.

"You sure you want to use that boy? He's a piece of shit. He'll fuck you if he gets the chance." Steve believed that he could scare me, a man who unemotionally stared a glock down without wincing.

"Man, I can handle this dude. He's not a problem. The problem is the group. I'll need more support."

"Yeah. Schmitty needs a guy to do undercover near 5th Street. Can you take care of that?"

I did not then nor now understand Steve's question. I wanted to start a case and work it to fruition. Steve was asking me to focus on things that did not involve my case, like I was not a real case agent.

"Naw, man. I'm going to focus on this job." I knew that he had to produce. I rejected a supervisor and a group to pursue individual goals. I am just doing what they always do, I thought. It's my turn to be a case agent. Let them do undercover.

The case progressed and blossomed into a huge continuing criminal enterprise. That is, the case was international in its scope. I had masterfully managed and utilized resources. One day, I was called into Steve's office for what he believed to be a 'keep doing a good job' talk.

"Hey, Maurice. How's it going partner." I gave a consenting nod and Steve continued.

M

"Listen. You have been transferred to a different group. I tried to keep you here but the big guy wanted you to go. All your cases will be reassigned and your snitches."

I felt betrayed and knew that I was being lied to. I heard the murmurings surrounding my denials to perform undercover. The 'I have a major case going' alibi did not bode well for me. I was supposed to do more. For four years, undercover was all I did. For four years I received the 'that a boy' pat on the back and praise for my exceptional ability to relate to drug dealers. I never viewed undercover successes as a gift from God. I was raised in the city and had a good handle on city life. It was easy. Writing reports was also easy; as was following chain of custody and handling arrest. The job was easy to me.

"Is this about not doing undercover? If it is, then that's fucked up, Steve. I have done undercover work hundreds of times. Why can't they work for me for a change?"

The emphasis I placed on "they" left little speculation in Steve's mind who he meant.

After jobs, Steve would buy pizza for the group and become an after the matter soothsayer. Light hearted conversation would ensue and briefly, group members would lower their guard and become true comrades. They always made me feel included because I was different. My ambition and naiveté would not allow me to notice that I was being used and not rewarded. Now that I lost my big case, my "baby", the revelation of truth twisted my stomach and watered his eyes.

Charles always told me to watch Steve. Charles knew Steve from the early 80's when they came on the job together. He watched Steve associated himself with known bigots. He watched Steve mature from an ignorant wanna be New York Italian gangster to a crafty, manipulative person empowered by a strong network of bigots that were notorious for justifying its racist beliefs. Charles was the elder statesman amongst the blacks in the office. He had been a 13 since 1987 but was not promoted to supervisory level. Everyone knew why but me, the FNG (fucking new guy). I avoided Charles because Steve told me to. "Damn guy can't even get promoted. He's an asshole." I accepted that as gospel.

"Maurice, you need to stop doing so much undercover and become a case agent. That's how you gonna get promoted. Not doing that bullshit that can get you killed. Hell, man, has a white boy done any undercover in your group?" Charles said, after pulling me to the side in the cafeteria one day. I thought about Charles' insight now. It was true. Not one white boy had done undercover.

"It's real easy, Maurice, to tell someone what to do when you're not on the frontline. You know what I'm saying?" he continued.

"Yeah, I hear you chief. Didn't you do a lot of undercover though?" I replied.

"You know what, you are young, dumb and full of cum. After you have stroked yourself enough, then what? Remember the narcotics officer that got killed two years ago. Remember the funeral. Everybody was there. You'll end up just like him, or worse. Those white boys will eat and use your ass up and ask for seconds."

I tried to think of a fate worse than death. Then I eluded Charles' eyes by bowing my head and shaking it in disbelief. How prophetic, I now thought.

"Thanks for the advice, Charles. You want something to drink?" I raised my head to find a disgusted Charles staring at me. I smiled. Charles left. I returned to the group and told Steve of my conversation with Charles. Steve laughed and told me not to worry.

"Nobody listens to him anyway."

****

ᴧᴧ

Tracey subtly glanced at me. Steve watched her. I felt like a corpse being attacked by lions and hyena.

"He won't tell us a thing, Tracey."

"What do you think he knows?"

They spoke in front of me as if I did not exist. Steve motioned to Tracey to follow him. They left the room. I waited. The door moaned once again and this time it was my attorney.

"You ready to go Maurice? They have nothing to hold you or Ronald on."

They picked him up too? I thought. Then he could not have given me up. If he did not, then who did?

"Yeah, let's go", I said anxious to leave.

Down the hall, Steve and Tracey were conversing. Actual, Steve was vigorously and insistently making his case. Tracey's ear was an obliging recipient. She just was not moved.

"Can we hold him or not. I want him charged. My guys got him going into the bar and intercepted him talking on the wire."

"What did he say, Steve?"

"Hell, you know how they talk with all that mumbo, jumbo language they use. The bottom line was that he knew about and transported money and drugs for the Harris organization."

"Ronald I may be able to charge later. We have independent information linking him to murders, drug deals and everything else. We need to tighten that up before we hold him. I can't hold Maurice or charge him with anything unless we get corroborative information. Wait, here he comes now."

By that time, my attorney and I left the room where I had been held and slugged down the hallway toward Tracey and Steve. I knew what they talking about.

"Leaving so soon, Maurice? You know one of these boys will flip on you. You know how they are."

"Fuck you saying, man?"

"Figure it out. I think we'll be seeing a lot of each other. Just like old times."

Tracey wanted to comfort and calm me with her touch, I could see it in her eyes, but it was not proper and it was too late.

"I've had enough of you, Steve. You fucked me already. What else do you want? You wouldn't let me work cases. You were the OPR investigator that tried to ruin my marriage. You were the one that screwed me. All I ever wanted was to…"

"You're a liar, Maurice," Steve darted

"That's enough, Steve," Tracey injected. Then she directed her attention to me.

"Don't leave town, Maurice. I'll contact you through your attorney. Okay?"

I glared at Tracey and realized she was trying her best to calm me. A tear track appeared on my face and the tear clung to my chin. This crying was becoming too familiar. When I was guilty I could not be charged. I recalled when I was innocent but found guilty. I hated Steve because Steve made me hate myself. I did not like what I had become.